Moonology™
Diary 2022

Yasmin Boland

HAY HOUSE

Carlsbad, California • New York City
London • Sydney • New Delhi

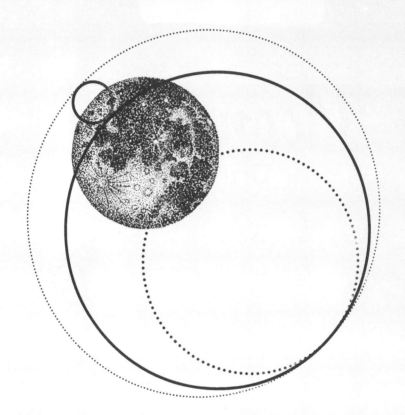

This diary belongs to

....

Published in the United Kingdom by:
Hay House UK Ltd, The Sixth Floor, Watson House,
54 Baker Street, London W1U 7BU
Tel: +44 (0)20 3927 7290; Fax: +44 (0)20 3927 7291
www.hayhouse.co.uk

Published in the United States of America by:
Hay House Inc., PO Box 5100, Carlsbad, CA 92018-5100
Tel: (1) 760 431 7695 or (800) 654 5126
Fax: (1) 760 431 6948 or (800) 650 5115; www.hayhouse.com

Published in Australia by:
Hay House Australia Pty. Ltd, 18/36 Ralph St, Alexandria NSW 2015
Tel: (61) 2 9669 4299; Fax: (61) 2 9669 4144 ; www.hayhouse.com.au

Published in India by:
Hay House Publishers India, Muskaan Complex, Plot No.3, B-2,
Vasant Kunj, New Delhi 110 070
Tel: (91) 11 4176 1620; Fax: (91) 11 4176 1630; www.hayhouse.co.in

A catalogue record for this book is available from the British Library.

ISBN: 978-1-78817-500-5

Interior images: vi: Shutterstock; 19: Jakkapan/123RF;
all other images Branding Darling/Etsy

Printed and bound in Italy by Graphicom

Contents

Welcome to 2022!

Let's start with some good news: this year, the most active of the big outer planets is... lucky Jupiter. In astrology and Moonology, the bigger, slower-moving, outer planets (Jupiter, Saturn, Uranus, Neptune and Pluto) provide the big backstory to whatever is going on. Within that backstory, the Moon triggers the different energies that move in and out of our lives.

You can think of it like this:

- The outer planets are like the hour hand on a clock.

- The Sun and the inner planets (Mercury, Venus and Mars) are like the minute hand.

- The Moon is like the second hand.

That might make it sound like the Moon is the least important, but that's absolutely not the case! The way it works in practice is that the inner and outer planets align with each other, and the Moon comes along and acts as a trigger that sets all the energies in motion.

This year, the Moon will trigger lots of lovely Jupiter action, which should take the world out of any slump and back to happier days. Jupiter is all about happiness and joy.

Looking at 2022, there are only three major planetary alignments, and they all happen in the first half of the year:

- In February, lucky Jupiter meets exciting Uranus.

- In April, expansive Jupiter meets meditative Neptune.

- In May, we get a meeting between amplifying Jupiter and passionate Pluto.

Planetary Alignments in More Detail

On 18 February, Jupiter aligns harmoniously with Uranus. Hopefully this will be a major (Jupiter) harbinger of change (Uranus). This alignment is about feel-good (Jupiter), evolution (Uranus), and the joy (Jupiter) of freedom (Jupiter/Uranus) – at last!

To put this in perspective: last year was characterized by a series of challenging alignments between Saturn (tough lessons) and Uranus (wake-up calls). We had a lot to deal with, including peak pandemic aftershocks. Thankfully, we're through that and, *hopefully*, into a much easier cycle. Hopefully? Put it this way, Aquarius (humanity) is hosting Saturn (lockdown) until 2023, so life is better but may not yet be 100 per cent back to the way it was before.

On the upside, 12 April (13 April Down Under) brings a wonderful alignment between Jupiter and Neptune, the planet of dreams and soul mates, meditation and illusion. An ideal outcome is that the world is going to wake up to the fact that spirituality and meditation are life-changers. If you're thinking about learning to meditate this year, follow that hunch. See my free guide, 'How to Meditate in Just 10 Steps', at moonologydiary.com.

Neptune is also about dreams, poetry and following your bliss, so let's hope this influence pans out in a way that's uplifting and inspiring (two very Neptunian words).

In mid-April, the Jupiter–Neptune alignment could also bring about some amazing opportunities for travel, big dreams, spiritual adventures, soul mate connections and massive manifestations.

However, it would be remiss of me not to mention that:

- the alignment between Jupiter and Neptune, which sees both planets on the same degree of the zodiac, is called a conjunction. This type of alignment can go either way: positively or negatively.

- Jupiter is known as, among other things, the 'lots of' planet: it amplifies.

- Neptune's negative side is all about illusion, deception and disappointment.

So, are you setting yourself up for lots of meditation, inspiration, bliss, poetry and big dreams of what you can do with your life, or are you heading for the negative side of Neptune? Neptune is the misty planet, and sometimes we can put our head in the Neptunian mist if we don't want to see something.

Then, on 3 May (4 May Down Under), there's a harmonious alignment between amplification planet Jupiter and powerful Pluto. Pluto is transformative, but also often brings about 'healing crises'. When it's troubled, it can be a very difficult energy. When it's challenging, Pluto energy is a darkness that takes us down so that we can better appreciate the light once we re-emerge. However, when

Pluto energy is positive, as it is in 2022, it's about releasing what's no longer working for us (and thereby making space for something that will).

There are no guarantees, but as Pluto is aligning with Jupiter, there really is huge scope (Jupiter) for the transformation of humanity from the inside out (Pluto) this year. That sounds very lofty, but it really is possible.

One way to harness these energies in 2022 would be to set your intentions now about what in your life you want to transform. Do it *now* if you feel ready, or come back to it later. Remember that Pluto works on a psychological level, so consider the mental state that you want to transform, as well as anything more tangible. For example, you might want to transform your mindset when it comes to money, rather than simply transform your bank account.

Pluto is also about throwing out the dead wood, so think about what you need to release in order to transform your life as we move through the first part of 2022.

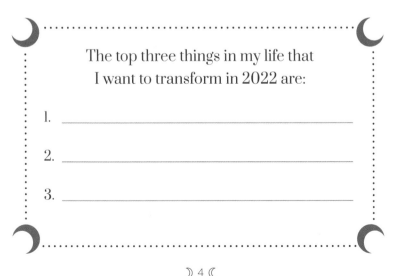

The top three things in my life that I want to transform in 2022 are:

1. _____

2. _____

3. _____

A last word about Jupiter: like all planets, Jupiter is constantly on the move through the 12 signs of the zodiac. This year it starts off in Pisces, moves into Aries in early May, goes retrograde back into Pisces in October and then takes up residence in Aries in December, where it'll stay well into 2023, marking the beginning of a new 12-year Jupiter cycle. Jupiter's movements will mean something different for everyone, and I'll go into more detail within the main diary as each move happens.

Retrogrades

A planet is said to go retrograde when it appears to reverse through the zodiac from our vantage point here on Earth. It's an optical illusion, with a lot of symbolic meaning, astrologically. You may have already heard of Mercury retrograde, which happens up to four times a year, though in fact all the planets appear to retrograde every year. As we move into 2022, it's a good idea to be aware of which planets will be retrograde, and when.

We start the year with the planet of love and abundance, Venus, retrograde. This means it's very much a time to be weighing up what we really value (though the start of any year is the ideal time to do this – agreed?). So do this now. Without thinking too hard about it, follow your gut feeling and on the next page write down the five most important people, places or situations in your life.

Once you've done that, you'll have a very clear idea of what is most important to you, and you can live 2022 prioritizing what matters most to you and what supports your values.

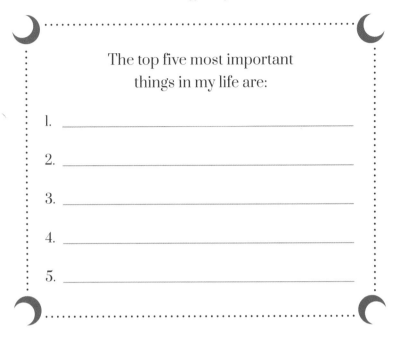

The top five most important
things in my life are:

1. _____

2. _____

3. _____

4. _____

5. _____

As mentioned, the best-known of the planetary retrogrades is surely Mercury retrograde. You could say we get three and a half of those this year (the half is because the last one starts in 2022 and ends in 2023). The dates are 14 January–3 February, 10 May–2 June, 9 September–2 October and 29 December–18 January 2023.

In October, Venus' counterpart, Mars, also goes retrograde, staying that way through most of January 2023. Mars is the engine of the zodiac – the planet that gets things done – so when Mars goes retrograde, it can feel like life is slowing down. As we all know, that can be a good thing as we get more time to invest heat and energy in a particular part of our lives depending on where Mars is retrograde in our birth charts. (If you don't already have a chart, you can get one for free at www.moonmessages.com/freechart.) However, when Mars goes retrograde it can also feel more difficult than usual to move forwards.

Overall, this means the period from January to around September is better for forging ahead than the months of October to December.

Eclipses

It's crucial to take eclipses into account when you're evaluating the overall energies of a year. In 2022, we have four eclipses and they're taking place in only two Star signs: Taurus and Scorpio. This means something different for everyone – but we all have Taurus and Scorpio in our chart somewhere. What's particularly interesting is that Taurus and Scorpio are opposite signs on the astrological wheel, so when the eclipses are happening one after the other, it's a bit like having the energies pinging across from each other and creating an electric current across that axis.

I like to think of eclipses as portals to another life. They open up opportunities and they close down what is no longer serving us. Most modern astrologers see eclipses as harbingers of change, doorways that open up like the hand of a higher power, which sees we're on the wrong path and (sometimes quite unceremoniously) shunts us onto our right and proper path, the one our soul signed up for before we were incarnated here on Earth.

Each eclipse will resonate in a particular House depending on your Star sign or Rising sign (*see pages 15–16 for A Quick Guide to the Houses*).

Here's a list of the two Houses that the Taurus–Scorpio eclipses will trigger for you. (For greater accuracy, use your Rising sign.)

- Aries or Aries Rising: 2nd and 8th Houses

- Taurus or Taurus Rising: 1st and 7th Houses

- Gemini or Gemini Rising: 12th and 6th Houses

- Cancer or Cancer Rising: 11th and 5th Houses

- Leo or Leo Rising: 10th and 4th Houses

- Virgo or Virgo Rising: 9th and 3rd Houses

- Libra or Libra Rising: 8th and 2nd Houses

- Scorpio or Scorpio Rising: 7th and 1st Houses

- Sagittarius or Sagittarius Rising: 6th and 12th Houses

- Capricorn or Capricorn Rising: 5th and 11th Houses

- Aquarius or Aquarius Rising: 4th and 10th Houses

- Pisces or Pisces Rising: 3rd and 9th Houses

Star Sign or Rising Sign?

Reading your Rising sign will give you a more accurate prediction than just reading your Star sign – the information is more like the forecast you'd get if you went to an astrologer for a personal reading. This is because your Rising sign is the most personal point on your chart, dictated not just by your date and time of birth but also by a third integer: your place of birth. You can discover your Rising sign (for free) at my site moonologydiary.com and I'd recommend you use your Rising sign for everything in this diary, particularly the information for the Houses at each New or Full Moon (look for 'What This Lunation Means for You'). Knowing your Rising sign means you'll tap into a much more powerful astrological message, trust me! That said, if you can't or don't want to find out your Rising sign, you can stick with just your regular Star sign.

Moonology for 2022

Now that we know the big planetary picture for 2022, what about the Moonology for the year ahead? Among the other events of the year, there are several headline acts to look out for:

- Super New Moon: 2 January in the northern hemisphere; 3 January in the southern hemisphere

- Black Moon (this is the second New Moon in a single calendar month): 30 April in the northern hemisphere; 30 May in the southern hemisphere

- Super Full Moon: 14 June

- Super Full Moon: 13 July

- Super New Moon: 23 December

Before we go any further, let's talk about the Moon and Her phases so that you have a context for these standout Moons and, importantly, the year's eclipses.

Many people ask whether this diary works for the northern or southern hemisphere. The answer is that it works for both!

The Phases of the Moon

It's worth knowing that the Moon goes through the same eight main phases, in the same order, every month: New Moon, Waxing Crescent Moon, First Quarter Moon, Gibbous Moon, Full Moon, Disseminating Moon, Third Quarter Moon and Balsamic Moon.

A lunar cycle lasts around 28 days and covers the time it takes for the Moon to complete one revolution around the Earth and to move through all eight phases and all 12 zodiac signs.

The waxing cycle includes those phases between New Moon and Full Moon, and the waning cycle includes phases from Full Moon back to New Moon.

Over the past few years I've also started working with a mysterious ninth phase, which is more to do with traditions other than straight astrology, but which I urge you to add into your Moon rituals. It occurs at the very end of the Balsamic phase and just before New Moon, and is known as the Dark Moon, when everything that has gone before can simply crumble away so you can enter the New Moon phase afresh.

Speaking broadly, here's an overview of energies and good actions to take during each phase:

	New Moon	This is the time to set your intentions. Not in an airy-fairy way, but really. It's the start of the lunar cycle and a time of new beginnings.
	Waxing Crescent Moon	Act on your intentions during this phase. It's pedal-to-the-metal time in terms of manifesting.
	First Quarter Moon	Challenges might arise at this time. All the better for you to recommit to your dreams.
	The Gibbous Moon	This Moon is stuffed full of emotions, dreams and wishes – and so are we.
	Full Moon	Emotional explosions are possible – you also see if your dreams are manifesting. Surrender to the Divine.
	Disseminating Moon	A time to process all you've been through, and to start letting go of anything you need to release.
	Third Quarter Moon	Allow what didn't work to fall away, so that you can move forward unencumbered.
	Balsamic Moon	A soothing time with powerful healing vibes. Make peace with life before the cycle of rebirth begins again at New Moon.

Working with the New and Full Moons

Now we get to what I consider the most fun part – using the Moon to create the life we want for ourselves. I'm a firm believer that one of the things we are on Earth to do is to learn to manifest, or consciously create. That includes creating our own reality, which is partly what this diary is about – making you aware of your superpowers and how to use them!

So how do we manifest? The short answer is: from the heart. You need to approach conscious creation from a good place, otherwise it can either backfire or just dissolve. Have you ever had the experience of being tantalizingly close to manifesting a dream when – poof! – it seemingly disappeared in a puff of reality? That happens mainly when we think something is 'too good to be true' or when we're manifesting from our ego-based mind rather than from our heart. Truly great manifesting comes from the heart and from our emotions, which is where the Moon comes in. Among the various things the Moon represents in astrology, one is emotion – making it the perfect conduit for our feelings.

One thing I hope you'll learn as you use this diary is to go right into your heart when you make your wishes and set your intentions each New Moon. Expressing your emotions as you wish makes all the difference.

When people first start to work with the Moon, they often focus on New Moon work and forget about forgiveness and release work at Full Moon. This has the powerful effect of clearing out our negativity, which is the most important thing to do to make our New Moon wishes come true.

The Full Moon marks the high point of the lunar cycle and is a time to make peace with ourselves, though it's also the most emotionally intense of all the Moon's phases. What better time to face all the feelings that come up? Acknowledge them, deal with them and process them at the time you feel them the most.

The work with both Moons combines to form the yin–yang of manifesting with the Moon. That's why I strongly want to encourage you to do Full Moon forgive-and-release work as much as you do New Moon wishes-and-intentions work. I truly believe it's why my methods work for me and for thousands of my readers and students around the world.

Wishing and Surrendering

We all know what it means to make wishes, but what does surrendering mean? The way I teach it, surrendering is about handing over to the Universe any wishes that haven't materialized, in case the Universe has a better idea. We do it once a month, at Full Moon.

But hang on – do I mean you ask the Universe for something at New Moon and then, if it doesn't happen, say

'Oh, never mind, it doesn't matter' at Full Moon? Not at all! To explain, let me tell you about buying our house, which took a seemingly interminable nine months from making our first offer to getting the keys. I think that's a pretty long time by anyone's standards. I believe one of the reasons it took so much time is because, while it was the right house for us, we weren't 100 per cent sure initially; it felt like such a big commitment and we wanted to keep our options open.

That likely slowed the process – confusion always slows manifesting. But our house waited for us to make up our minds, because every New Moon I'd set the intention to buy the house, and every Full Moon, when we still hadn't bought it or any other house, I'd surrender it to the Divine, knowing that nothing meant for us would pass us by.

Several months into the process we realized that we really, truly did want the house and that it was meant for us. Owing to the amount of time the process took, and due to fluctuating house prices at the time, we ended up buying the house with very happy hearts and for a great price. It couldn't have worked out better, and when we finally got the keys I realized what all that waiting and surrender and intention and surrender had been about!

So come on a journey with me this year. Working with the Moon like this truly can help you create the life you're dreaming of. But it has to come from the heart. With our house, for example, I wanted to find the perfect place for the people I love most – my family. Come from the heart when you manifest and you'll never go wrong! Working with the Moon will also help you to feel more connected to the planet, which is good for your nervous system and for maintaining positive mental health.

A Quick Guide to the Houses

Over the course of the year, the Moon will touch every aspect of our lives, which are represented in one or other of the Houses, or sectors, in our birth chart. For example, the 7th House is effectively your Love Zone; the 10th House is your Career and Ambitions Zone; and the 12th House is the deepest and darkest part of your chart.

In every month of the diary, the New Moon and Full Moon sections reveal 'What This Lunation Means for You' and list each of the 12 Star signs alongside a numbered House. Once you know which House is being triggered for you, refer to the following page to see what it means.

New Moons offer the chance to make a new start, whereas Full Moons bring conclusions. So a New Moon in your 2nd House, for example, might indicate a time when a new start in your finances presents itself to you. A Full Moon in your 2nd House could bring about the climax or culmination of a financial cycle (hopefully for the better!).

Here is a brief summary of what's governed by each House. You can find more detailed information, including an explainer video, on my site (moonologydiary.com).

The 1st House: your appearance and image; self-identity; how you come across to others.

The 2nd House: cash, property and possessions; values, including how you value yourself.

The 3rd House: communication; siblings; neighbours; quick trips; early learning and education.

The 4th House: home and family; all things domestic; where you belong; your past.

The 5th House: romance; creativity; kids (your own or someone else's); pursuit of pleasure; love affairs.

The 6th House: daily routines, including at work; your health; duty.

The 7th House: your lovers, your spouse and your ex; open enemies; any sort of partner, including business partners; cooperation and competition.

The 8th House: joint finances; credit cards; debts; sex; anything you consider taboo; inheritance; transformation.

The 9th House: study; travel; the search for meaning and to understand Life; higher learning; spirituality; dreams.

The 10th House: your career and ambitions; how you make your mark on the world; what you're known for.

The 11th House: friends; networks; social circles; the Internet; hopes and wishes.

The 12th House: the deepest, darkest, most sensitive part of your chart. Your fears; your spirituality; self-undoing; withdrawal; secret or hidden enemies.

How to Use This Diary

You'll see that each month begins with a two-page overview, followed by daily diary space for you to write in. Some people use these pages as an agenda or to record important dates and appointments, while others note their feelings or what they're grateful for on any given day.

At the time of each New or Full Moon, you'll find information about which Star sign the lunation is taking place in, what this means for you and how to harness the cosmic energies. At New Moon there's space to write your wishes, intentions and goals, and at Full Moon, make sure you write your all-important Forgiveness and Release list – and then burn it. If you're reluctant to rip pages out, write your list on a separate sheet of paper and burn that instead.

I've included some amazing Sanskrit Moon mantras in this year's diary. I learned about these at the ashram in India I've been visiting for nearly 20 years, and I consider it a blessing to be able to pass them on to you.

The Signs of the Zodiac

As the Moon moves through the sky, She passes through all 12 signs of the zodiac every month. On the diary pages for each day of the year, you'll see an astrology symbol to denote which zodiac (or Star) sign the Moon is in on that day. When you see two glyphs, it means the Moon transitions from the first sign to the second on that day.

Aries	♈	Libra	♎
Taurus	♉	Scorpio	♏
Gemini	♊	Sagittarius	♐
Cancer	♋	Capricorn	♑
Leo	♌	Aquarius	♒
Virgo	♍	Pisces	♓

On the dates of the New and Full Moons, I've included the degrees at which each lunation occurs. If you think of the zodiac as a circle of 12 signs, each sign represents 30° of the full 360° chart. Each degree is further divided into 60 minutes, which are expressed from 0–59. So, for instance, the notation 12°Cp20 means that the lunation occurs at 12° and 20 minutes in Capricorn.

This diary will guide you through your Moon work in the year ahead, and I've created a special page at my site moonologydiary.com (**password: 2022**) where you can access even more resources to boost your Moon practices.

I've received so many emails from readers of the *Moonology Diary*, and the message that comes through again and again is 'Thank you! Working with the Moon has changed my life for the better. This stuff works.' And so it does! Find out for yourself in 2022.

Weekly
Diary

JANUARY

M	T	W	T	F	S	S
					1	2
3	4	5	6	7	8	9
10	11	12	13	14	15	16
17	18	19	20	21	22	23
24	25	26	27	28	29	30
31						

FEBRUARY

M	T	W	T	F	S	S
	1	2	3	4	5	6
7	8	9	10	11	12	13
14	15	16	17	18	19	20
21	22	23	24	25	26	27
28						

MARCH

M	T	W	T	F	S	S
	1	2	3	4	5	6
7	8	9	10	11	12	13
14	15	16	17	18	19	20
21	22	23	24	25	26	27
28	29	30	31			

APRIL

M	T	W	T	F	S	S
				1	2	3
4	5	6	7	8	9	10
11	12	13	14	15	16	17
18	19	20	21	22	23	24
25	26	27	28	29	30	

MAY

M	T	W	T	F	S	S
						1
2	3	4	5	6	7	8
9	10	11	12	13	14	15
16	17	18	19	20	21	22
23	24	25	26	27	28	29
30	31					

JUNE

M	T	W	T	F	S	S
		1	2	3	4	5
6	7	8	9	10	11	12
13	14	15	16	17	18	19
20	21	22	23	24	25	26
27	28	29	30			

JULY

M	T	W	T	F	S	S
				1	2	3
4	5	6	7	8	9	10
11	12	13	14	15	16	17
18	19	20	21	22	23	24
25	26	27	28	29	30	31

AUGUST

M	T	W	T	F	S	S
1	2	3	4	5	6	7
8	9	10	11	12	13	14
15	16	17	18	19	20	21
22	23	24	25	26	27	28
29	30	31				

SEPTEMBER

M	T	W	T	F	S	S
			1	2	3	4
5	6	7	8	9	10	11
12	13	14	15	16	17	18
19	20	21	22	23	24	25
26	27	28	29	30		

OCTOBER

M	T	W	T	F	S	S
					1	2
3	4	5	6	7	8	9
10	11	12	13	14	15	16
17	18	19	20	21	22	23
24	25	26	27	28	29	30
31						

NOVEMBER

M	T	W	T	F	S	S
	1	2	3	4	5	6
7	8	9	10	11	12	13
14	15	16	17	18	19	20
21	22	23	24	25	26	27
28	29	30				

DECEMBER

M	T	W	T	F	S	S
			1	2	3	4
5	6	7	8	9	10	11
12	13	14	15	16	17	18
19	20	21	22	23	24	25
26	27	28	29	30	31	

January

This is an interesting year, due to there being so few big planetary events – there are just three major planetary alignments and only four eclipses. So, are we in for a calmer year? Let's hope so!

January starts off well compared with the past few years, which hopefully is a good sign for the whole year. It brings a New Moon almost straight away, on 2 January, which is perfectly timed for making new year's resolutions if you haven't done so already. Make them just after the New Moon, and if you can, join me on my Facebook page for a free New Moon session. Remember that 2022 starts with Venus already retrograde, so New Year is a good time to re-evaluate *everything*. If you didn't fill out the 'Top five most important things in my life' checklist on page 6, do it now to decide your priorities for the year.

Venus being retrograde can make some people feel a bit detached from their partner. If that's you right now, don't worry; it's a good chance to see if you've been taking each other for granted and to re-evaluate your love life overall. If you're experiencing Venus retrograde as a delay in expected funds, hold on – the cork will finally pop out of the money bottle at the end of the month.

Also note that in mid-January Mercury goes into one of four retrograde cycles it has in store this year.

There's a lot of looking backwards as the year begins, but just go with it. It must be what we all need before we start tearing forwards!

M	T	W	T	F	S	S
31					1	2
3	4	5	6	7	8	9
10	11	12	13	14	15	16
17	18	19	20	21	22	23
24	25	26	27	28	29	30

~ Things to do this month ~

1. Re-evaluate your life – take a fearless inventory!
2. Contact someone you need to sort things out with.
3. Set your professional goals for 2022.

Super New Moon in Capricorn

Place	Date	Time
London	2 January	18:33
Sydney	3 January	05:33
Los Angeles	2 January	10:33
New York	2 January	13:33

If you had to choose an ideal way for a year to kick off, at least for people who know they create their own reality, then the January 2022 planetary line-up would have to be a contender. We get the New Moon on 2 or 3 January (depending on where you are in the world), which already is a very auspicious start because the New Moon is the ideal time to let the Universe know your intentions and desires, your wishes and dreams, and this time it's happening as the whole year kicks off.

If you're on the spiritual path – and you almost certainly are if you bought this diary – you'll know that this is the perfect time to make a 12-month plan. Take a moment to write a letter to yourself as though it were the end of the year. What are you proud of having achieved? Start with the words 'Dear [your name], Wow! What a year! I'm so proud of you for...' Fill in what you know your soul wants you to achieve, whether your goal is material, emotional or spiritual. By setting out your intentions now, at the time of the New Moon, you will be tapping into the collective consciousness which is all about this amazing new start we get once a year.

Also, this particular New Moon is taking place just before a beautiful alignment between Venus and Neptune, which is absolutely perfect for dreams, summoning soul mates, envisaging the money you need in order to be comfortable, and so on. Whatever you do, start 2022 by tapping into the New Moon this month.

⚵ What This Lunation Means for You

To discover where the energy of this New Moon is for you, find your Star sign or Rising sign here, see which House is involved, and then read A Quick Guide to the Houses (*see pages 15–16*): Aries – 10th House; Taurus – 9th House; Gemini – 8th House; Cancer – 7th House; Leo – 6th House; Virgo – 5th House; Libra – 4th House; Scorpio – 3rd House; Sagittarius – 2nd House; Capricorn – 1st House; Aquarius – 12th House; Pisces – 11th House.

● New Moon Mantra ●

Om Namo Bhagavate Kurma Devaya Namaha.

This mantra honours the planet Saturn, the ruler of the sign of Capricorn. You can listen to it at moonologydiary.com.

New Moon Wishes and Intentions

My current biggest, most audacious goal, wish or intention at this New Moon is:

_____

Now turn it into an affirmation.

Write it here as if it has already happened:

_____

I commit to reciting this affirmation, with conviction, multiple times a day for the next month.

Sign here:

_____

Now add three micro-goals for this month that feed into your main goal:

_____

_____

_____

My other wishes, intentions and goals for this month, and action points I can take towards them, are:

1. My goal/wish/intention:

_____

The action I will take to make this happen:

_____

_____

2. My goal/wish/intention:

_____

The action I will take to make this happen:

_____

_____

3. My goal/wish/intention:

_____

The action I will take to make this happen:

_____

_____

Bring it home with a visualization ceremony.
Visit moonologydiary.com for a visualization audio meditation.

December Week 52

27 Monday ♎

28 Tuesday ♎ ♏ ♐

29 Wednesday ♏ ♐

30 Thursday ♏ ♐ ♐

 ♐

Friday 31

♐♑

Saturday 1

♑

Sunday 2

Super New Moon occurs at 12°Cp20
London   18:33
Los Angeles 10:33
New York   13:33

This Week

We get a New Moon on the second day of 2022, perfectly
timed for us to make some super-powerful New Moon
intentions as we tap into the collective consciousness
of people doing the same thing all around the world.

January Week 1

3 Monday

Super New Moon occurs at 12°Cp20
Sydney   05:33

4 Tuesday

5 Wednesday

6 Thursday

♓

Friday **7**

 ♓ ♈

Saturday **8**

 ♈

Sunday **9**

What are you grateful for right now?

This Week

It's a New Moon week, so – without wanting to pressure
you – it's time to hit the ground running with plans, dreams
and schemes for how you want your 2022 to play out.

January Week 2

....

10 Monday

....

11 Tuesday

....

12 Wednesday

....

13 Thursday

....

○ ♊   Friday 14

Mercury goes retrograde (until 4 February).

○ ♊ ♋   Saturday 15

○ ♋   Sunday 16

This Week

To add to the start-of-the-year fun, which has
offered up a New Moon and a retrograde Venus,
this week sees Mercury go retrograde too. If you
want to give your life a do-over, now is the time.

Full Moon in Cancer

Place	Date	Time
London	17 January	23:48
Sydney	18 January	10:48
Los Angeles	17 January	15:48
New York	17 January	18:48

Welcome to the first Full Moon of 2022. Every Full Moon is a chance to move on from the past, but the first Full Moon of the year is that plus-plus – agreed? The astrology for 2021 was pretty intense, so if you've emerged from last year in one piece, now is the time to be grateful. Thankfully, this year's astrology is a little easier.

Think now about what you're leaving behind. What didn't work out in 2021 as you wanted and left you feeling 'less than'? That's what you want to release. Years are man-made constructs but they're quite useful for drawing a line under the past, and now is the time to do just that.

This particular Full Moon in Cancer has an especially healing element to it, thanks to an alignment between the planet of the mind, Mercury, and the healing planetoid Chiron. So put on some 528 Hz or 963 Hz music (easily found on the Internet) and get ready to release. In particular, let go of any dramas you've had in relation to work or family, or in that juggling trick known as a work-life balance. There could be some quick shifts related to love or abundance for people who are able to just let go.

Remember to forgive anyone and anything from 2021, and before, that has upset you. Full Moon forgiveness releases karmic ties, which keep us stuck in a cycle. Hanging on to negative feelings such as anger does no one any good. Instead, acknowledge what happened, forgive it, release it and move on.

☿ What This Lunation Means for You

To discover where the energy of this Full Moon is for you, find your Star sign or Rising sign here, see which House is involved, and then read A Quick Guide to the Houses (*see pages 15–16*): Aries – 4th House; Taurus – 3rd House; Gemini – 2nd House; Cancer – 1st House; Leo – 12th House; Virgo – 11th House; Libra – 10th House; Scorpio – 9th House; Sagittarius – 8th House; Capricorn – 7th House; Aquarius – 6th House; Pisces – 5th House.

☿ Releasing 2021 and Welcoming 2022

This first Full Moon of 2022 turns a page on the past. A wonderful way to move on from all that you've been through is to make a list titled 'What I am releasing' Note down any experiences that you're still upset or traumatized about, and then... burn the list (burning it is powerful on an energetic level). Then replace what you've released by making a list titled 'What I am OH so grateful for!' Be expansive!

Full Moon Forgiveness and Release List

Every month we need to work on forgiving and releasing so that we can move on. This month in particular, think about who and what you need to forgive in your family, your childhood and your current home life. We also need to release resistance to whatever is holding us back. For example, if your New Moon goal was to get in better shape, you might need to release resistance to exercise!

Make a list of what you want to forgive and release, then ideally burn it (use a separate sheet of paper if you prefer). Join me (for free) in a fire ceremony on Facebook (see moonmessages. com/fbevents).

I forgive/release:

_____

_____

_____

_____

_____

⚴ Questions to Ask at This Full Moon

Have I allowed my working life to impact negatively my personal life (or vice versa)? If so, what should I do about it?

_____

_____

_____

_____

Have I been acting too tough lately? How has that impacted my most important relationships and what can I do to make this better?

_____

_____

_____

Who do I most need to have a healing conversation with, why, and how can I make that happen this month?

_____

_____

_____

_____

January Week 3

....

17 Monday   ♋ ○

Full Moon occurs at 27°Cn50
London   23:48
Los Angeles   15:48
New York   18:48

....

18 Tuesday   ♋♌ ○

Full Moon occurs at 27°Cn50
Sydney   10:48

....

19 Wednesday   ♌ ○

....

20 Thursday   ♌♍ ○

....

◐♍ Friday **21**

◐♍♎ Saturday **22**

◐♎ Sunday **23**

This Week

As soon as the Full Moon has been and gone, we
move into the Moon's waning cycle, which runs
from Full Moon back to New Moon – the time to
relax and just 'be', as much as you possibly can.

January Week 4

24 Monday ♎

....

25 Tuesday ♎ ♏

....

What are you grateful for right now?

....

26 Wednesday ♏

....

27 Thursday ♏ ♐

....

Friday **28**

Saturday **29**

Venus retrograde ends.

Sunday **30**

This Week

Mercury and Mars both move into Capricorn this week, so you'll have extra oomph in whichever House Capricorn is in for you (*see pages 15–16*). If you'd like to know more about your Houses, please read the 'Houses' guide at my site, moonologydiary.com.

February

So what does Valentine's month 2022 bring us? Forgive me if you think Valentine's is for saps, because I love it. When I was single, I was always super-curious to see what the vibes around that day would be, and even now that I'm married to my beloved and very romantic Frenchman, I still check it out each year to see what it might bring.

So, here's the news for all the lovers out there: Valentine's Day 2022 looks amazing! For a start, the Moon will be in the shiny, showy sign of Leo, which is great energy for making a show of how much you appreciate someone. Plus, Valentine's comes at the very end of the Moon's waxing cycle, so emotions will be rising – and what's Valentine's without emotions, after all?

Valentine's Day comes just before the Moon in Leo becomes Full, which, as long as you don't let pride get in your way on 14 February, should augur well for making us all feel like romantic rock stars. What's more, Valentine's is taking place just before a truly perfect Venus–Mars meeting. Venus and Mars are the lovers of the zodiac – the girlfriend and boyfriend, if you like (though absolutely not restricted to heterosexual relationships) – so having them meeting up just after Valentine's is ideal. And if you're single? For one thing, it's a great year to get some friends together to go out and have some fun – there's more to Valentine's than kissing. Back in my single days, if I didn't go out with friends to celebrate life on Valentine's Day, I might have used the night to make a love vision board with my BFF. Try it! (Turn to page 181 to discover how it's done.)

M	T	W	T	F	S	S
	1 ●	2	3	4	5	6
7	8 ◐	9	10	11	12	13
14	15	16 ○	17	18	19	20
21	22	23 ◑	24	25	26	27
28						

~ Things to do this month ~

1. Get back on track.
2. Make massive changes.
3. Take up yoga or another spiritual practice.

New Moon in Aquarius

Place	Date	Time
London	1 February	05:45
Sydney	1 February	16:45
Los Angeles	31 January	21:45
New York	1 February	00:45

Here's a solid, new start if ever there was one: the New Moon this month is taking place pretty much on top of the strong and stable planet Saturn, so if you've begun 2022 feeling a bit out of control, this is the New Moon to commit to getting back on track. If you're feeling confined, though, watch out, because that feeling could be exacerbated. Just know that whatever is going on in your life right now is happening so that you learn something important.

Mercury is retrograde at the time of the New Moon, so it could well be that you're still being asked to learn a lesson you should have learned a while ago. On a macro level, it could be that whatever is happening in the world right now is taking place because we have a collective lesson to learn.

Every month is a great month to make New Moon wishes and to write down your intentions, but this month that's true more than ever, because bossy planner Saturn is involved. In particular, think about the commitments you're making to yourself. If you feel trapped or blocked, work out why and how you can get around whatever is in your way.

⚵ What This Lunation Means for You

To discover where the energy of this New Moon is for you, find your Star sign or Rising sign here, see which House is involved, and then read A Quick Guide to the Houses (*see pages 15–16*): Aries – 11th House; Taurus – 10th House; Gemini – 9th House; Cancer – 8th House; Leo – 7th House; Virgo – 6th House; Libra – 5th House; Scorpio – 4th House; Sagittarius – 3rd House; Capricorn – 2nd House; Aquarius – 1st House; Pisces – 12th House.

⚵ Love Is in the Air

In honour of Valentine's month, try this spell by San Francisco-based white witch and Wicca teacher Francesca De Grandis, author of *Be a Goddess!* Jump in the shower and lather up from head to toe. As you wash, say to yourself: *I am washing away my blocks to love – I am good enough, beautiful enough, to be loved.* Repeat the process if you feel you have a lot of clearing to do.

● New Moon Mantra ●

Om Hram Prajapataye Namah.

This mantra honours Saturn, the traditional ruler of the sign of Aquarius. You can listen to it at moonologydiary.com.

New Moon Wishes and Intentions

My current biggest, most audacious goal, wish or intention at this New Moon is:

_____

Now turn it into an affirmation.

Write it here as if it has already happened:

_____

I commit to reciting this affirmation, with conviction, multiple times a day for the next month.

Sign here:

_____

Now add three micro-goals for this month that feed into your main goal:

_____

_____

_____

My other wishes, intentions and goals for this month, and action points I can take towards them, are:

1. My goal/wish/intention:

_____

The action I will take to make this happen:

_____

_____

2. My goal/wish/intention:

_____

The action I will take to make this happen:

_____

_____

3. My goal/wish/intention:

_____

The action I will take to make this happen:

_____

_____

Bring it home with a visualization ceremony.
Visit moonologydiary.com for a visualization audio meditation.

Jan/Feb Week 5

31 Monday

New Moon occurs at 12°Aql9
Los Angeles 21:45

1 Tuesday

New Moon occurs at 12°Aql9
London   05:45
Sydney   16:45
New York   00:45

Festivals of Imbolc (northern hemisphere) and Lammas (southern hemisphere)

2 Wednesday

3 Thursday

Friday 4

Mercury retrograde ends.

Saturday 5

Sunday 6

This Week

Here's a fun little fact you might not know: the New Moon in Aquarius always heralds Chinese New Year. This time around, we're going into the Year of the Tiger.

February Week 6

7 Monday

....

8 Tuesday

What are you grateful for right now?
....

9 Wednesday

....

10 Thursday

....

Week 6 February

◐ ♊♋   Friday 11

○ ♋   Saturday 12

○ ♋   Sunday 13

This Week

This is a week when Mercury (communication) and
Pluto (power) are getting together, so make powerful
communications (both written and spoken) your aim.

Full Moon in Leo

Place	Date	Time
London	16 February	16:56
Sydney	17 February	03:56
Los Angeles	16 February	08:56
New York	16 February	11:56

There's something very exciting about this Full Moon. For one thing, it takes place in the fiery sign of Leo. Full Moons are always intense, but even more so when they're 'on fire'! This year, the Full Moon is taking place just ahead of one of the signature alignments of 2022: a Jupiter–Uranus link, which heralds a harmonious alliance.

Full Moons are also turning points. Once they've been and gone, we move from the intent-laden waxing cycle to the surrendering spirit of the waning cycle. Surrender doesn't mean giving up; it means handing everything over to the Divine. We're all Divine, whether we realize it or not, so when we hand over anything to the Divine, effectively that includes the part of us which is Divine, too.

To decode this at the time of the Full Moon in Leo, we must surrender and release pride (Leo is where we're proud; we all have Leo in our charts). And then, having let go and entrusted our life, wishes, problems – everything – to the Divine (or to the Universe, God or your goddess), guess what? We allow space for changes to happen.

Remember, Uranus is prominent right now, and Uranus is all about chaos and ceding control. This is a week when changes really are possible, so use the Full Moon to give up any need you have to control. Go on – just do it!

⚹ What This Lunation Means for You

To discover where the energy of this Full Moon is for you, find your Star sign or Rising sign here, see which House is involved, and then read A Quick Guide to the Houses (*see pages 15–16*): Aries – 5th House; Taurus – 4th House; Gemini – 3rd House; Cancer – 2nd House; Leo – 1st House; Virgo – 12th House; Libra – 11th House; Scorpio – 10th House; Sagittarius – 9th House; Capricorn – 8th House; Aquarius – 7th House; Pisces – 6th House.

⚹ Release Control

Have you been very controlling recently? Have you been micro-managing? Have you been so intent on trying to make life go your way that you've forgotten how to let go and trust the Divine? Be honest. If the answer to any of these questions is 'yes', I offer you my favourite Full Moon mantra: *Om Namo Narayani.* It's one I learned in India and it's used all over the country. The words are Sanskrit and mean: 'I surrender to the Divine.' If you only ever use one mantra, use this one, and especially at Full Moon. It changed my life in the most amazing ways and it can change yours too! Try it this waning cycle.

Full Moon Forgiveness and Release List

This month we need to release pride and control. Pride is associated with Leo, and no wonder: Leo is represented by the lion – the Lord of the Jungle, the King and Queen, the ruler and the Sun, around which we all spin. Write down anything you've done due to pride or ego so you really acknowledge it, then forgive yourself for it. Also, release resistance to doing things for your ego's sake. What are you doing or not doing because you want to look good or you're worried about not looking good? Work on that!

I forgive/release:

_____

_____

_____

_____

_____

_____

_____

☿ Questions to Ask at This Full Moon

What would I do if I knew I couldn't fail?

_____

_____

_____

_____

When was the last time I danced like no one was watching –
literally and metaphorically? Have I been too uptight, and, if
so, how could I work on that?

_____

_____

_____

Which of my talents, assets or personality traits am I most
proud of? _(It's okay to be proud of yourself, as long as you also
stay humble.)_

_____

_____

_____

_____

February Week 7

----

14 Monday

----

15 Tuesday

----

16 Wednesday

Full Moon occurs at 27°Le59
London   16:56
Los Angeles   08:56
New York   11:56

----

17 Thursday

Full Moon occurs at 27°Le59
Sydney   03:56

○ ♍   Friday 18

○ ♍ ♎   Saturday 19

○ ♎   Sunday 20

This Week

Valentine's Day can be amazing for people in a loving
relationship but less so for people who aren't. If
you're single, reach out to a friend this 14 February
and have some of the fun only singles can!

February Week 8

21 Monday ♎ ♏ ◑

22 Tuesday ♏ ◑

23 Wednesday ♏ ♐ ◐

What are you grateful for right now?

24 Thursday ♐ ◑

Friday 25

Saturday 26

Sunday 27

This Week

If one of your 2022 new year's resolutions was to do yoga, Tai Chi or anything along those lines, use this week to make good on that promise to yourself. A Mars–Neptune link supports any spiritual practices.

March

March brings a biennial meeting of the planet of anger, Mars, and the planet of fury, Pluto. In other words, if you're in a bad mood as March begins, or if you're around someone who's grumpy, watch out! (If you know your astrology chart, check to see if you have a Mars–Pluto link because this event is going to affect you more than most.)

Overall, the first week of March is going to be a bit of a minefield, thanks to this Mars–Pluto clash. However, there's also a lot of magic in this alignment, so if you're into conscious manifesting, it's a week to dig deep as you throw out your 'I am!' statements. These are simply affirmations of who you want to be. For example, 'I am a bestselling author!' if you're writing a book that you have big ambitions for; or 'I am the mother of a super-happy family!' if you're trying to conceive or you want more harmony at home, and so on.)

March also brings an energy that allows for amazing self-transformation. If you need courage to shed the old you, now is the time to do the work. That includes making affirmations like the above, visualizing where you want to be and feeling what it's like to have your wishes fulfilled. (Note, this is less about wanting, say, a new car, and more about wanting to better yourself. Pluto is involved and is more about the intangible than the tangible.)

Also note that the second half of the month sees a clash between fiery Mars and electric Uranus, so it's a month to master your temper if you're prone to outbursts!

M	T	W	T	F	S	S
	1	2 ●	3	4	5	6
7	8	9	10 ◐	11	12	13
14	15	16	17	18 ○	19	20
21	22	23	24	25 ◐	26	27
28	29	30	31			

~ Things to do this month ~

1. Make some magic.
2. Breathe through anger.
3. Transform your life.

New Moon in Pisces

Place	Date	Time
London	2 March	17:34
Sydney	3 March	04:34
Los Angeles	2 March	09:34
New York	2 March	12:34

Pisces is the mystical sign, all about dreams and soul mates, poetry and intuition. Think of the bottom of the sea, perhaps near a rocky coast. Sometimes it's cool, dark and unfathomable down there and sometimes glorious shafts of light magically break through from the surface – when this happen you start to get a sense of the depths of Pisces. This New Moon gives us a chance to work on that deeper part of ourselves – our more mystical side. If the New Moon takes place during waking hours for you, it's a marvellous New Moon to meditate your way through.

Pisces is also a visionary sign, making this a peak conscious-manifesting period, too. Be sure to make your wishes and affirmations, and practise your visualizations, and notice how they feel. If they feel good, you're on the right path. This New Moon is in the same place as lucky Jupiter, so we have Lady Luck on our side. Make the most of it!

Under this New Moon there's a lovely link between loving and abundant Venus and the planet of action, Mars. So if your dreams are to do with making love more often, attracting more love or friendship, or drawing more abundance to yourself, you most certainly have the stars on your side.

✳ What This Lunation Means for You

To discover where the energy of this New Moon is for you, find your Star sign or Rising sign here, see which House is involved, and then read A Quick Guide to the Houses (*see pages 15–16*): Aries – 12th House; Taurus – 11th House; Gemini – 10th House; Cancer – 9th House; Leo – 8th House; Virgo – 7th House; Libra – 6th House; Scorpio – 5th House; Sagittarius – 4th House; Capricorn – 3rd House; Aquarius – 2nd House; Pisces – 1st House.

✳ Meditate, Meditate, Meditate

It's not easy to be disciplined enough to meditate every day, but it's oh so worth it. If you don't have a meditation practice yet, use the energy from the New Moon in Pisces to find one. Try one of the many apps available, or one of the many wonderful meditation videos on YouTube.

● New Moon Mantra ●

Om Vam Varunaya Nahaha.

This mantra honours the traditional Pisces-ruling planet, Jupiter. Listen to it at moonologydiary.com.

New Moon Wishes and Intentions

My current biggest, most audacious goal, wish or intention at this New Moon is:

_____

Now turn it into an affirmation.

Write it here as if it has already happened:

_____

I commit to reciting this affirmation, with conviction, multiple times a day for the next month.

Sign here:

_____

Now add three micro-goals for this month that feed into your main goal:

_____

_____

_____

My other wishes, intentions and goals for this month, and action points I can take towards them, are:

1. My goal/wish/intention:

_____

The action I will take to make this happen:

_____

_____

2. My goal/wish/intention:

_____

The action I will take to make this happen:

_____

_____

3. My goal/wish/intention:

_____

The action I will take to make this happen:

_____

_____

Bring it home with a visualization ceremony.
Visit moonologydiary.com for a visualization audio meditation.

Feb/March Week 9

28 Monday

1 Tuesday

2 Wednesday

New Moon occurs at 12°Pi06
London   17:34
Los Angeles 09:34
New York   12:34

3 Thursday

New Moon occurs at 12°Pi06
Sydney   04:34

Mars meets Pluto – *kapow!*

Friday 4

Saturday 5

Sunday 6

This Week

It's a week to be very mindful of your temper.
If you start to get upset, back off and breathe –
for the sake of everyone concerned! Make any
anger a stepping stone to transformation.

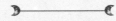

March Week 10

7 Monday

8 Tuesday

9 Wednesday

10 Thursday

What are you grateful for right now?

☽ I ♋   Friday 11

☽ ♋   Saturday 12

☽ ♋ ♌   Sunday 13

Peak meditation day.

This Week

It's an especially good week for meditation, thanks
to the annual Sun–Neptune conjunction, so make
sure you take time out just to say, 'Ommm...'!

Full Moon in Virgo

Place	Date	Time
London	18 March	07:17
Sydney	18 March	18:17
Los Angeles	18 March	00:17
New York	18 March	03:17

Astrology is actually a bit of a keywords game: once you understand the keywords for the various signs, planets and Houses, you start to understand how astrology works. Some of the keywords for Virgo, which is the sign for the Full Moon this month, include 'chaste', 'reliable' and 'modest'. So you might expect the Full Moon in Virgo to be rather mild-mannered. However, that's not really the case now as this year's Full Moon in Virgo is taking place in alignment with the planet of getting down-and-dirty, Pluto.

Pluto has been quite active lately, making this a very transformative period (and we're not even in the eclipse season yet!). 'Transformation' is a Pluto keyword, which is why you'll keep reading it in this diary. As I've mentioned before, with Pluto the transformations are often more psychological than material or physical. I mention this because it's important to know that even if there are no tangible effects, there are often intangible ones. As we go into this Full Moon, think about how you can transform the way you show up in the world every day and how you're serving the world. Every successful New Age teacher will tell you that it's when you flip from 'What's in it for me?' to 'How can I serve?' that your message starts getting out into the wider world.

This is also a good Full Moon for releasing any tendencies you have to being either too critical of others or – arguably even worse – too critical of yourself.

⚆ What This Lunation Means for You

To discover where the energy of this Full Moon is for you, find your Star sign or Rising sign here, see which House is involved, and then read A Quick Guide to the Houses (*see pages 15–16*): Aries – 6th House; Taurus – 5th House; Gemini – 4th House; Cancer – 3rd House; Leo – 2nd House; Virgo – 1st House; Libra – 12th House; Scorpio – 11th House; Sagittarius – 10th House; Capricorn – 9th House; Aquarius – 8th House; Pisces – 7th House.

⚆ Forgive, Forgive and Forgive Again

Recite my 'Forgiveness Formula on Full Moon Night', speaking from your heart: *'Under the glorious Full Moon, I forgive everything, everyone, every experience, every memory of the past or present that needs forgiveness. I forgive positively everyone. I also forgive myself for past mistakes. The Universe is love, and I'm forgiven and governed by love alone. Love is now adjusting my life. Realizing this, I abide in peace.'*

Full Moon Forgiveness and Release List

The Full Moon is when all our emotions come up, so it's the right time to process them. In particular, the Full Moon is a great time to allow any darker feelings we've been suppressing to be illuminated, before releasing them into the ether. Once you start to do this, your life truly will change. So, who are you forgiving this Full Moon?

I forgive/release:

_____

_____

_____

_____

_____

_____

_____

_____

⚹ Questions to Ask at This Full Moon

Have I been too picky lately, if so with whom and could that be an unnecessary source of tension?

_____

_____

_____

How do I feel about forgiving? Can I see that forgiving someone doesn't make what they did right, but allows me to release and move on?

_____

_____

_____

_____

Who have I been too critical of – myself or someone else? What about? How can I stop?

_____

_____

_____

_____

March Week 11

....

14 Monday

....

15 Tuesday ♌○

....

16 Wednesday ♌♍○

....

17 Thursday ♍○

....

 ♍ ♎   Friday 18

Full Moon occurs at 27°Vi40

London	07:17
Sydney	18:17
Los Angeles	00:17
New York	03:17

◯ ♎   Saturday 19

◯ ♎ ♏   Sunday 20

Spring Equinox/Ostara (northern hemisphere)

This Week

Mind how you go this week. On the one hand, there's
celestial space for some loving forgiveness and
relationship-mending, but there's also room for hurting
the people we love most. Live and love consciously!

March Week 12

....

21 Monday

....

Autumn Equinox/Mabon (southern hemisphere)
....

22 Tuesday

....

23 Wednesday

....

24 Thursday

....

 ♑ Friday **25**

What are you grateful for right now?

 ♑ Saturday **26**

⬤♑♒ Sunday **27**

This Week

If you start to feel like there isn't enough love or money to go around this week, take a breath. You're just feeling an alignment between loving Venus and cold, hard Saturn, and this too shall pass! Make a plan instead.

April

This month brings two New Moons, on the first and last days of the month. The first New Moon is in Aries, marking the start of a new lunar cycle, since Aries is the first sign of the zodiac. If you haven't got into your New Moon practice so far in 2022, now is the time to start!

The second New Moon (known as a Black Moon) is an eclipse in the sign of Taurus, which augurs well for the world economy. For those who know their birth chart, it's also good for you personally if you have any planets or points in your chart around 10° Taurus or Scorpio.

Mid-month we get an amazing – awe-inspiring, even – meeting between Jupiter and Neptune. Jupiter is the planet of expansion and higher learning, and Neptune is the planet of the Divine and of poetry, soul mates and meditation, so this could be a month when we humans move a little bit further along the evolutionary path. It would be nice to think this link represents a time of more poetry, lots of meditation and plenty of inspiration. However, there's a more confusing side to misty Neptune; it can also be about disappointment, deception and disillusionment. The connection this month harks back to 2009, as it's more or less the end of a cycle that began then.

In astrology, we always have choices: you can tap into the inspiration and use it to take your personal meditation practice higher (or to start a practice if you don't yet have one); or you can look for disappointment in your life and blame Jupiter–Neptune. I know which choice I'll be making!

M	T	W	T	F	S	S
				1 ●	2	3
4	5	6	7	8	9 ◐	10
11	12	13	14	15	16 ○	17
18	19	20	21	22	23 ◑	24
25	26	27	28	29	30 ●	

~ Things to do this month ~

1. Take up or keep doing meditation.
2. Write some inspired poetry or prose.
3. Restart financially.

New Moon in Aries

Place	Date	Time
London	1 April	07:24
Sydney	1 April	17:24
Los Angeles	31 March	23:24
New York	1 April	02:24

Aries is the first sign of the zodiac. Among other things, it represents the 'Me! Me! Me!' of the zodiac (and remember we all have Aries in our chart somewhere). It's also the sign from which all the other signs flow. It marks the start of new life, new shoots and new plants, and, in the northern hemisphere, the end of the long, cold winter and the start of spring. It's the beginning.

When you take an interest in astrology, you learn that you have two, or even three, new year's days in your lexicon: New Year's Day on 1 January; the move of the Sun into Aries around 22 March (this date varies each year); and the New Moon in Aries which takes place in late March or April.

Even though January marks the official start of the year, the New Moon in Aries is the date that marks the start of the new year for me. You might prefer to think of it as a second new year or a second chance at new year. Either way, it's here now so set some intentions and make some wishes! If you need to heal, set intentions around that as the healing energy around the 2022 New Moon in Aries is super-strong.

✳ What This Lunation Means for You

To discover where the energy of this New Moon is for you, find your Star sign or Rising sign here, see which House is involved, and then read A Quick Guide to the Houses (*see pages 15–16*): Aries – 1st House; Taurus – 12th House; Gemini – 11th House; Cancer – 10th House; Leo – 9th House; Virgo – 8th House; Libra – 7th House; Scorpio – 6th House; Sagittarius – 5th House; Capricorn – 4th House; Aquarius – 3rd House; Pisces – 2nd House.

✳ Happy Astrological New Year!

One of the things I hope you'll come to understand by using this diary is the power of intention; the idea that by setting intentions, you're far more likely to realize your goals. With this month's New Moon in the first sign of the zodiac, Aries, we're being offered a chance to start over again. And let's not forget about the New Moon eclipse – it's the perfect time to set your financial intentions for the year ahead.

● New Moon Mantra ●

Om Namo Bhagavate Narasimhaya Namaha.

This mantra honours Mars, the ruling planet of Aries. You can listen to it at moonologydiary.com.

New Moon Wishes and Intentions

My current biggest, most audacious goal, wish or intention at this New Moon is:

_____

Now turn it into an affirmation.

Write it here as if it has already happened:

_____

I commit to reciting this affirmation, with conviction, multiple times a day for the next month.

Sign here:

_____

Now add three micro-goals for this month that feed into your main goal:

_____

_____

_____

My other wishes, intentions and goals for this month, and action points I can take towards them, are:

1. My goal/wish/intention:

_____

The action I will take to make this happen:

_____

_____

2. My goal/wish/intention:

_____

The action I will take to make this happen:

_____

_____

3. My goal/wish/intention:

_____

The action I will take to make this happen:

_____

_____

Bring it home with a visualization ceremony.
Visit moonologydiary.com for a visualization audio meditation.

March Week 13

---

28 Monday

---

29 Tuesday

---

30 Wednesday

---

31 Thursday
New Moon occurs at 11°Ar30
Los Angeles 23:24

 Friday 1

New Moon occurs at 11°Ar30

London	07:24
Sydney	17:24
New York	02:24

Saturday 2

Sunday 3

This Week

This year's Aries New Moon takes place on April Fool's Day. Don't worry, though: there's no astrological significance and it won't affect your intentions. More importantly, make this month's wishes while remaining mindful that we're in a new cycle.

April Week 14

4 Monday

5 Tuesday

Be extra nice!

6 Wednesday

7 Thursday

Friday **8**

Saturday **9**

What are you grateful for right now?

Sunday **10**

This Week

This could be a tough week for you if you're
currently battling authority. For best results, make
'I channel my energy wisely' your mantra.

Full Moon in Libra

Place	Date	Time
London	16 April	19:55
Sydney	17 April	04:55
Los Angeles	16 April	11:55
New York	16 April	14:55

Libra is the relationship-oriented sign of the zodiac, so this Full Moon provides a yardstick for how well our relationships are going. If you've been forcing a relationship, this might be the time it blows up. If you're in a newish relationship and all is going well, now might be when you take it to the next level. If you're in an established relationship, think of it as another notch on your relationship belt.

This year's Full Moon in Libra is extra lovely. It takes place ahead of some beautiful and harmonious alignments between Mercury, Venus and Uranus, so happy love events may happen quickly now – romance is in the air!

The only concern is that the Full Moon itself is clashing with Pluto, so if there are issues in one of your most important relationships, then they need attention. There could be power struggles, which get no one anywhere, so live consciously and intentionally. If you're in a relationship with a lot of negativity, now is also the time to deal with that. Whatever happens now could bring about a crisis, but one that may prove to be healing, one way or another.

Pluto is also the detox planet, so work through any toxicity now so it becomes easier to express your feelings. You may even want to give the person you care about a lovely surprise.

✳ What This Lunation Means for You

To discover where the energy of this Full Moon is for you, find your Star sign or Rising sign here, see which House is involved, and then read A Quick Guide to the Houses (*see pages 15–16*): Aries – 7th House; Taurus – 6th House; Gemini – 5th House; Cancer – 4th House; Leo – 3rd House; Virgo – 2nd House; Libra – 1st House; Scorpio – 12th House; Sagittarius – 11th House; Capricorn – 10th House; Aquarius – 9th House; Pisces – 8th House.

✳ A Relationship Mini-Inventory

Tap into the power of the Full Moon in Libra to think about your love life and what you need to do to get it on track:

One thing I need to clear with my partner or ex: ....

....

One thing about .... (someone who matters to you) *that I need to be more grateful for:* ....

....

Based on this, this week I am going to ....

....

Full Moon Forgiveness and Release List

It's Full Moon, so it's time for forgiving and releasing. It's important to remember that forgiveness includes forgiving ourselves, not just others. If we don't forgive ourselves, we end up feeling unworthy, which blocks positive manifestations. This month, think about who you need to forgive in your most important relationships, and then think about mistakes you feel you've made, in relationships past and present, and forgive yourself! Write it all down, using a separate sheet of paper if you want to, as ideally you should then burn it. Join me (for free) in a fire ceremony on Facebook (see moonmessages. com/fbevents).

I forgive/release:

_____

_____

_____

_____

_____

_____

⚹ Questions to Ask at This Full Moon

Which past relationship left me completely 'undone'? Can I forgive everything that happened so I can go on to achieve true future happiness?

_____

_____

_____

Is there someone in my life I want to know better? What could I do to vibe with the Full Moon and reach out to them this month? _(Ideally, do this just before Full Moon.)_

_____

_____

_____

Who do I need to have a loving conversation with, and what do I need to say?

_____

_____

_____

_____

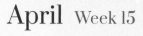

April Week 15

....

11 Monday

....

12 Tuesday

....

13 Wednesday

....

14 Thursday

....

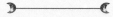

Week 15 **April**

◯ ♎︎   Friday **15**

◯ ♎︎   Saturday **16**
Full Moon occurs at 26°Li45
London   19:55
Los Angeles   11:55
New York   14:55

◯ ♎︎ ♏︎   Sunday **17**
Full Moon occurs at 26°Li45
Sydney   04:55

This Week

This week's Jupiter–Neptune alignment makes now
the time to dream (Neptune) big (Jupiter). Write
down your dreams, recite them as affirmations
and visualize them as being reality.

April Week 16

18 Monday ♏︎↗ ○

19 Tuesday ♏︎↗ ♐︎ ○

20 Wednesday ♐︎ ☾

21 Thursday ♐︎ ♑︎ ○

Friday 22

Saturday 23

What are you grateful for right now?

Sunday 24

This Week

There are some super-intense planetary alignments
this week, which could lead to power struggles and
upsets. Your best bet is simply not to get involved.

New Moon Eclipse in Taurus

Place	Date	Time
London	30 April	21:28
Sydney	1 May	06:28
Los Angeles	30 April	13:28
New York	30 April	16:28

This is a very exciting, highly charged New Moon eclipse. It takes place in the sign of Taurus, which is all about values, comforts and finances. Taurus is represented by the bull, which happens to be the symbol of Wall Street, so if you want to make some changes to your finances, this is the month to set your intentions around that.

In case you need to hear this: there's nothing wrong with wanting the money you need to live a comfortable life with the people you love most! We humans are incarnated here on planet Earth to experience what life in 3D has to offer us, to learn how to create and how to enjoy life in its physicality. You've undoubtedly heard the idea that 'We are not human beings. We are spiritual beings having a human experience!', and whether you want money to spend on yourself, your family or friends, or to help others, money is a part of that experience.

If you currently want to make money, working online is a superb idea because the planet Uranus, which rules technology, is in Taurus. The first step is to decide what you have to offer that people need. Ask yourself, from your heart: *How may I serve the world?* Allow the answer you get to be your guide.

The planet Uranus also helps us to bring about sudden change and even radical reversals, and it's being triggered this month, by Mars. Hopefully this will be a wonderful blessing; Mars–Uranus makes it much easier than usual to take radical action.

✳ What This Lunation Means for You

To discover where the energy of this New Moon is for you, find your Star sign or Rising sign here, see which House is involved, and then read A Quick Guide to the Houses (*see pages 15–16*): Aries – 2nd House; Taurus – 1st House; Gemini – 12th House; Cancer – 11th House; Leo – 10th House; Virgo – 9th House; Libra – 8th House; Scorpio – 7th House; Sagittarius – 6th House; Capricorn – 5th House; Aquarius – 4th House; Pisces – 3rd House.

● New Moon Mantra ●

Om Namo Bhagavate Para Surama Ya Namaha.

This mantra honours Venus, ruler of the sign of Taurus. You can listen to it at moonologydiary.com.

New Moon Wishes and Intentions

My current biggest, most audacious goal, wish or intention at this New Moon is:

_____

Now turn it into an affirmation.

Write it here as if it has already happened:

_____

I commit to reciting this affirmation, with conviction, multiple times a day for the next month.

Sign here:

_____

Now add three micro-goals for this month that feed into your main goal:

_____

_____

_____

My other wishes, intentions and goals for this month, and action points I can take towards them, are:

1. My goal/wish/intention:

_____

The action I will take to make this happen:

_____

_____

2. My goal/wish/intention:

_____

The action I will take to make this happen:

_____

_____

3. My goal/wish/intention:

_____

The action I will take to make this happen:

_____

_____

Bring it home with a visualization ceremony.
Visit moonologydiary.com for a visualization audio meditation.

April Week 17

....

25 Monday

....

26 Tuesday

....

27 Wednesday

....

28 Thursday

....

 ♑︎

Friday **29**

● ♑︎ ♉︎

Saturday **30**

New Moon eclipse occurs at 10°Ta28
London   21:28
Los Angeles 13:28
New York   16:28

● ♉︎

Sunday **1**

New Moon eclipse occurs at 10°Ta28
Sydney   06:28

Festivals of Beltane (northern hemisphere) and Samhain (southern hemisphere)

This Week

Don't underestimate the power of this week's New Moon
eclipse to help shunt you into a new financial reality.
Chances like this really don't come along very often.

May

There's so much going on astrologically this month! Firstly, an alignment between Jupiter and Pluto means there's a lot (Jupiter) of power and magic (Pluto) in the air. There's a chance for positive changes now, many of which could relate back to the extraordinary events of 2020, when Jupiter and Pluto started what's called a new synodic cycle. These two planets are slow-moving and meet less often than the faster planets, so their alignments are a big deal. In this case, they bring an epic chance for transformation on a personal, generational and societal level. Where do you invite transformation into your life?

Secondly, Jupiter is changing signs. Barring retrogrades, this happens only about once every 12 months, so it's a big deal. Jupiter is the planet of luck, expansion, adventure and all good things. The House being triggered now by Jupiter and where you're getting extra luck, or perhaps where you're going to make a bid for freedom, is the same House that the New Moon in Aries triggered for you (*see page 81*).

As if it wasn't enough to have Jupiter and Pluto meet and for Jupiter to change signs, we also get a Full Moon eclipse. More about this as May unfolds, but if you want to live consciously and intentionally, think about what in your life you're holding on to that you know has to be released. Letting go of your own free will will make your life a lot easier than if you hang on.

M	T	W	T	F	S	S
						1
2	3	4	5	6	7	8
9	10	11	12	13	14	15
16	17	18	19	20	21	22
23	24	25	26	27	28	29
30	31					

~ Things to do this month ~

1. Decide that you're lucky – count your blessings.
2. Identify where in your life change is needed.
3. Release something that's no longer working for you.

May Week 18

. . . .

2 Monday

. . . .

3 Tuesday

. . . .

4 Wednesday

. . . .

5 Thursday

. . . .

 Friday **6**

 Saturday **7**

Sunday **8**

What are you grateful for right now?

This Week

We're now in the eclipse season, so be particularly aware of what you're doing and how this impacts what you've decided to create.

May Week 19

9 Monday ♌ ♍ ◗

10 Tuesday ♍ ◗

Mercury goes retrograde (until 3 June).

11 Wednesday ♍ ◗

12 Thursday ♍ ♎ ◯

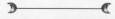

○ ♎   Friday **13**

○ ♎ ♏   Saturday **14**

○ ♏   Sunday **15**

Full Moon eclipse occurs at 25°Scl7
Los Angeles   21:14

This Week

We're now on the brink of the Full Moon eclipse,
so the energies are high. Note that the energies
of Full Moon eclipses are at their most powerful
when you accept and release what needs to go.

Full Moon Eclipse in Scorpio

Place	Date	Time
London	16 May	05:14
Sydney	16 May	14:14
Los Angeles	15 May	21:14
New York	16 May	00:14

The first idea that springs to mind looking at this eclipse is to let go – let go of all the ****; let go of whatever upset and angst you're holding on to; let go of resentment and fear; let go of anyone or anything you're clinging on to for dear life. Release the number-one thing you're scared to release. Not just because 'If you let it go and it comes back, it's yours – and if it doesn't, it probably never was,' as the old saying goes; but also because, every now and then, we have to look at where we've developed a toxic attachment or fear and we need to work through it.

One thing you'll start to learn as you move along the spiritual path is that fear only has the power we give it. This Full Moon is brilliant for giving us a safe space to process our fears. One of the best ways to do this is through the process of tapping (*see below*). Full Moons are always the time to let go and this one even more so, since it's an eclipse in the sign of Scorpio, which sometimes holds on rather grudgingly.

⯛ What This Lunation Means for You

To discover where the energy of this Full Moon is for you, find your Star sign or Rising sign here, see which House is involved, and then read A Quick Guide to the Houses (*see pages 15–16*): Aries – 8th House; Taurus – 7th House; Gemini – 6th House; Cancer – 5th House; Leo – 4th House; Virgo – 3rd House; Libra – 2nd House; Scorpio – 1st House; Sagittarius – 12th House; Capricorn – 11th House; Aquarius – 10th House; Pisces – 9th House.

⯛ Try tapping

Tapping, or the Emotional Freedom Technique (EFT), involves tapping on certain points on the head and body to help release stress. It's super-powerful because it allows us to face our fear, and it nearly always starts with acknowledging whatever it is we're dealing with – no spiritual bypassing here! The idea is that we work through our feelings: we feel them, we accept them and, in doing so, we release them. For this week's exercise I asked my good friend, tapping expert Anna Maria Aicher, to create a video to help you tap away fear and upsets. You can watch it (for free) on my site, moonologydiary.com. If you haven't tried tapping yet, give it a go; it feels incredible!

Full Moon Forgiveness
and Release List

This Full Moon is particularly good for forgiveness because this month it's the sign of Scorpio, and no sign holds on to a grudge more than Scorpio (and we all have Scorpio somewhere in our charts). So, this month think of someone you've held a grudge against for too long. (Maybe you can hardly remember the reason!) Include them in your Forgiveness List – write this on a separate sheet of paper if you prefer, because ideally you should now burn it. Join me (for free) in a fire ceremony on Facebook (see moonmessages.com/fbevents).

I forgive/release:

_____

_____

_____

_____

_____

_____

_____

✳ Questions to Ask at This Full Moon

Have I been holding on to upsets lately? If so, what good has it done me?

_____

_____

_____

Is there someone who has a grudge against me? If so, why, and can I extend the hand of friendship? Is there someone I've been mad with for too long who I can make up with?

_____

_____

_____

_____

Am I comfortable with acknowledging my shadow side and working with it?

_____

_____

_____

_____

May Week 20

---

16 Monday

Full Moon eclipse occurs at 25°Scl7

London   05:14
Sydney   14:14
New York   00:14

♏⚲♐ ○

---

17 Tuesday

♐ ○

---

18 Wednesday

♐♑ ○

---

19 Thursday

♑ ○

Friday **20**

Saturday **21**

Sunday **22**

What are you grateful for right now?

This Week

As the Full Moon eclipse takes place, it moves
us out of the eclipse season and into the
waning cycle. It's time to breathe out.

May Week 21

23 Monday

24 Tuesday

25 Wednesday

26 Thursday

 Friday **27**

● ♉ Saturday **28**

● ♉♊ Sunday **29**

This Week
At the end of this week, we get the first New Moon since the eclipse season. Life could feel quite different now. Commit to a restart in at least one part of your life.

New Moon in Gemini

Place	Date	Time
London	30 May	12:30
Sydney	30 May	21:30
Los Angeles	30 May	04:30
New York	30 May	07:30

This New Moon brings second chances to people who need them. It's taking place in Gemini, which is the sign associated with communication and the mind – think writing, listening, books, reading, talking, thinking – so it's a great time to sort out our communication skills.

How well are you getting your message across? If you're sending out mixed messages, you'll get back mixed results. If you talk yourself down, you'll feel down; others will also think less of you, because if you sound like you don't value yourself, then why should anyone else value you? How we communicate with others, about who we are and what we want, has a big impact on our lives.

As the New Moon in Gemini takes place, Gemini's planet, Mercury, is retrograde. This creates an opportunity to rethink any previous communications that didn't have the desired outcome. Maybe you need to backtrack on something you said, or try again to have that tricky conversation? Mercury retrograde ends a couple of days after the New Moon, so do the work on the way you communicate now, and you can move mountains.

In Australia and New Zealand this is also a Black Moon, i.e. the second New Moon in a calendar month.

✳ What This Lunation Means for You

To discover where the energy of this New Moon is for you, find your Star sign or Rising sign here, see which House is involved, and then read A Quick Guide to the Houses (*see pages 15–16*): Aries – 3rd House; Taurus – 2nd House; Gemini – 1st House; Cancer – 12th House; Leo – 11th House; Virgo – 10th House; Libra – 9th House; Scorpio – 8th House; Sagittarius – 7th House; Capricorn – 6th House; Aquarius – 5th House; Pisces – 4th House.

✳ Chant to Release Your Throat

Simply chant (out loud or silently) the famous meditation word 'Ommm', which is said to be the sound the Universe makes. As you do so, imagine a blue light at your throat to represent your throat chakra. A healthy throat chakra means a healthy communication channel.

● New Moon Mantra ●

Om Namo Bhagavate Buddha Devaya Namaha.

This mantra honours the planet Mercury, ruler of the sign of Gemini. You can listen to it at moonologydiary.com.

New Moon Wishes and Intentions

My current biggest, most audacious goal, wish or intention at this New Moon is:

_____

Now turn it into an affirmation.

Write it here as if it has already happened:

_____

I commit to reciting this affirmation, with conviction, multiple times a day for the next month.

Sign here:

_____

Now add three micro-goals for this month that feed into your main goal:

_____

_____

_____

My other wishes, intentions and goals for this month, and action points I can take towards them, are:

1. My goal/wish/intention:

_____

The action I will take to make this happen:

_____

_____

2. My goal/wish/intention:

_____

The action I will take to make this happen:

_____

_____

3. My goal/wish/intention:

_____

The action I will take to make this happen:

_____

_____

Bring it home with a visualization ceremony.
Visit moonologydiary.com for a visualization audio meditation.

May/June Week 22

30 Monday

New Moon occurs at 09°Ge03
London   12:30
Sydney   21:30
Los Angeles 04:30
New York   07:30

31 Tuesday

1 Wednesday

2 Thursday

Friday 3

Saturday 4

Sunday 5

This Week

The New Moon this week marks a time to clear your head and start all over again. It'll soon be time to act upon the ideas that have come to you during Mercury retrograde.

June

Every now and then, we get a month when it seems like the skies are on our side – or, at least, are giving us a bit of a break. After the eclipse seasons, with the recent Mercury retrograde thrown in, June brings that relief. There are no eclipses, no major planetary clashes and Mercury ends its retrograde cycle on the third of the month. So, all in all, life should be a little bit easier for the coming four weeks.

An important note, however: Saturn is retrograde now, which is kind of a good thing. Think of it like this: generally, Saturn is the planet of karma and rolls around our charts over a period of 30 years, teaching us the heavy life lessons our souls need to take on. Saturn is the Great Teacher of the zodiac, but instead of being the teacher everyone loves, Saturn is the teacher many fear – yet also the teacher we look back on and think, 'Yeah, that mean old thing really taught me a few lessons I needed to learn.'

That's when Saturn is moving forwards. When Saturn goes retrograde, as it's doing now, it brings a sort of break from the relentless learning and maturing, and we get a chance to think about the lessons we've learned. However, if there has been a major drama in your life in the past few months, it could be that it'll resurface during the retrograde, so you can ensure you really did learn all you were meant to. That said, given that Saturn is also the building planet, Saturn *retro*-grade – when the planet appears to reverse – also heralds a time to *re*-build.

M	T	W	T	F	S	S
		1	2	3	4	5
6	7 ◑	8	9	10	11	12
13	14 ○	15	16	17	18	19
20	21 ◑	22	23	24	25	26
27	28	29 ●	30	31		

~ Things to do this month ~

1. Consider what you've learned.
2. Stop spinning your wheels.
3. Be constructive.

June Week 23

6 Monday

7 Tuesday

What are you grateful for right now?

8 Wednesday

9 Thursday

○ ♎ ♏ Friday 10

○ ♏ Saturday 11

○ ♏ ♐ Sunday 12

This Week

This week sees a link between loving and abundant
Venus and crazy Uranus, so radical changes to do with
love and abundance may be heading your way.

Super Full Moon in Sagittarius

Place	Date	Time
London	14 June	12:51
Sydney	14 June	21:51
Los Angeles	14 June	04:51
New York	14 June	07:51

The Full Moon in Sagittarius is always a great time to take a step back and see how far you've come in life. No matter what's been going on for you this year, on one level or another, you've evolved. Even if you feel like you've been quite stagnant, you're not the same person you were when the year began. So look back and see what you've achieved over the past 12 months. Take some time to appreciate your accomplishments. Are there any risks you've taken that have paid off?

This Full Moon is a particularly benevolent one, taking place in the fun sign of Sagittarius. Straight after the Full Moon we get an alignment between Mars and the planetoid Chiron, which is all about healing – sexual and otherwise.

So, make the night of the Full Moon super-special with your beloved. And if you're single? The Full Moon is always a good time to be out with friends, as the energies are high. Plus, it's a great time to do any healing work around the male and the masculine – in other words, if you've had issues because of a male in your life and you're ready to forgive them and move on, do it now.

✶ What This Lunation Means for You

To discover where the energy of this Full Moon is for you, find your Star sign or Rising sign here, see which House is involved, and then read A Quick Guide to the Houses (*see pages 15–16*): Aries – 9th House; Taurus – 8th House; Gemini – 7th House; Cancer – 6th House; Leo – 5th House; Virgo – 4th House; Libra – 3rd House; Scorpio – 2nd House; Sagittarius – 1st House; Capricorn – 12th House; Aquarius – 11th House; Pisces – 10th House.

✶ Look How Far You've Come

Make a timeline of your life, going back as far as you can remember. Note when you started and finished school, fell in love for the first time (and broke up), and so on. The idea is to get the big picture of your life so you can see how you've evolved as a person. Sagittarius energy is very expansive, and the Full Moon in Sagittarius makes now a great time to treat life as an adventure and review your journey so far – including your darkest times. I keep a list like this on my computer so I can add to or refer to it any time I want.

Full Moon Forgiveness and Release List

As we do our forgiving and releasing work this month, it could be the ideal time to focus on forgiving yourself. It's so important to do this every now and then. We all mess up, and if we can be as good-humoured about it as we are when our friends or kids mess up, we're on the way to self-love. Also this month, think about forgiving things that happened to you at school that scarred you in some way. Join me (for free) on Facebook where I'll be doing a Full Moon fire ceremony (see moonmessages.com/fbevents).

I forgive/release:

_____

_____

_____

_____

_____

_____

_____

⚹ Questions to Ask at This Full Moon

Can I forgive that person who hurt me when I was at school?
What would be the benefit of forgiving them now?

_____

_____

_____

Can I commit to taking a 'glass half full' approach to life for the
whole of the coming four weeks? What do I need to be more
optimistic about, and why?

_____

_____

_____

Am I doing at least one form of movement that's good for my
body, mind and spirit, like yoga, Tai Chi or dance? If not, which
one might I take up, and what is the reason for my choice?

_____

_____

_____

_____

June Week 24

13 Monday ♐ ○

14 Tuesday ♐♑ ○

Super Full Moon occurs at 23°Sg25
London   12:51
Sydney   21:51
Los Angeles   04:51
New York   07:51

15 Wednesday ♑ ○

16 Thursday ♑♒ ○

○ ♒   Friday 17

○ ♒ ♓   Saturday 18

○ ♓   Sunday 19

This Week

If you've never done yoga before, try it this week (as sporty Mars and healing Chiron meet). And if you already do yoga, practise every day this week!

June Week 25

· ·

20 Monday

· ·

21 Tuesday

Summer Solstice/Litha (northern hemisphere);
Winter Solstice/Yule (southern hemisphere)
What are you grateful for right now?

· ·

22 Wednesday

· ·

23 Thursday

· ·

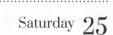 Friday **24**

Saturday **25**

 Sunday **26**

This Week

Love is in the air this week, thanks to a
powerful connection between loving Venus and
passionate Pluto. Show someone you care.

New Moon in Cancer

Place	Date	Time
London	29 June	03:52
Sydney	29 June	12:52
Los Angeles	28 June	19:52
New York	28 June	22:52

This end-of-June New Moon is a powerful one and we can more or less choose which of its vibrations we want to tune in to. The first two alignments forming after the New Moon (and therefore flavouring it) are vastly different from each other. First, we have a loving, beautiful and joyous link between Venus and Jupiter. Venus cares while Jupiter amplifies, so there's a lot of love around under such a planetary combination. However, this is somewhat challenged by the clash of angry Mars with eruptive Pluto, which is also demanding our attention.

You could say this lunation comes down to a fight for your attention – so, where are you focused? If you're focused on the good things in life, it should be a sweet time with a lot of room for showering your loved ones with more love. If you're finding life a bit tough right now, it could be that you feel the love less and the Mars–Pluto anger more.

What you tune in to here depends on your chart. If Pluto clashes with one of the planets on your chart, you'll find it hard not to tune in to the Mars–Pluto clash. Everyone else can focus on the good stuff! The most important thing is to honour your feelings and live consciously.

⚴ What This Lunation Means for You

To discover where the energy of this New Moon is for you, find your Star sign or Rising sign here, see which House is involved, and then read A Quick Guide to the Houses (*see pages 15–16*): Aries – 4th House; Taurus – 3rd House; Gemini – 2nd House; Cancer – 1st House; Leo – 12th House; Virgo – 11th House; Libra – 10th House; Scorpio – 9th House; Sagittarius – 8th House; Capricorn – 7th House; Aquarius – 6th House; Pisces – 5th House.

⚴ Healing Ancestral Wounds

This is a great time to study your lineage and honour your ancestors. Who came before you and what gifts did they bestow on you? Knowing where you came from is empowering and illuminating. If you learn of trauma in your own or your family's past, this New Moon is a powerful time to make the decision to heal it with love and acceptance.

● New Moon Mantra ●

Om Namo Bhagavate Vasu Devaya Namaha.

This mantra honours the Moon, which is associated with the sign of Cancer. You can listen to it at moonologydiary.com.

New Moon Wishes and Intentions

My current biggest, most audacious goal, wish or intention at this New Moon is:

_____

Now turn it into an affirmation.

Write it here as if it has already happened:

_____

I commit to reciting this affirmation, with conviction, multiple times a day for the next month.

Sign here:

_____

Now add three micro-goals for this month that feed into your main goal:

_____

_____

_____

My other wishes, intentions and goals for this month, and
action points I can take towards them, are:

1. My goal/wish/intention:

_____

The action I will take to make this happen:

_____

_____

2. My goal/wish/intention:

_____

The action I will take to make this happen:

_____

_____

3. My goal/wish/intention:

_____

The action I will take to make this happen:

_____

_____

Bring it home with a visualization ceremony.
Visit moonologydiary.com for a visualization audio meditation.

June Week 26

. . . .

27 Monday

. . . .

28 Tuesday

New Moon occurs at 07°Cn22
Los Angeles 19:52
New York   22:52

. . . .

29 Wednesday

New Moon occurs at 07°Cn22
London   03:52
Sydney   12:52

. . . .

30 Thursday

. . . .

Week 26 **July**

 Friday **1**

● ♌ Saturday **2**

 Sunday **3**

This Week

It's an amazing time to do a clear-out of your house.
Removing clutter frees you from the past. Ask the
classic Marie Kondo question of each object – 'Does
it spark joy?' – and keep or donate it on that basis.

July

This month kicks off with a super-intense alignment between angry Mars and furious Pluto, so don't be alarmed if you feel like July isn't going to be your best month as it begins. There's just some 'stuff' that we all need to clear out and process. So, whatever is making you feel angry or feisty – or, if you're lucky, especially driven – as July begins, this is the issue to turn your attention to.

These challenging energies will settle down quite quickly, but don't wish the first week of the month away. Rather, think of it as a healing process that can cleanse something from your life that's become toxic.

Communication planet Mercury is super-active this month, putting the focus on talking things through, or writing them down, to sort them out. The good news is that most of the alignments that Mercury is making this month are positive and harmonious, so any efforts to clear up miscommunications should be rewarded with clarity.

There are also some lovely Venus links to watch out for. Venus is the planet of love and abundance, so when She's well placed it augurs well for the whole world! On 6 July She harmonizes with the healer planetoid Chiron, so any upsets from the start of the month can be healed. With Chiron, it's often about the 'talking cure', so speak your truth with love.

On 13 July Venus connects with serious Saturn, making the middle of the month the ideal time to have important talks about your romantic future and to ink any deals.

Note that the last week of July is quite intense, thanks to some planetary clashes, so go easy – if someone provokes you, take care not to snap back!

M	T	W	T	F	S	S
				1	2	3
4	5	6	7 ◑	8	9	10
11	12	13 ○	14	15	16	17
18	19	20 ◑	21	22	23	24
25	26	27	28 ●	29	30	31

~ Things to do this month ~

1. Talk, talk, talk.
2. Say sorry and mean it.
3. Feeling wound up? Try boxing!

July Week 27

4 Monday ♍ ○

5 Tuesday ♍♎ ○

6 Wednesday ♎ ◑

7 Thursday ♎ ◑

What are you grateful for right now?

Friday **8**

 Saturday **9**

Sunday **10**

This Week

It's a week of healing, and if you don't say too much,
too soon, it's possible to turn around a situation
that's been going in the wrong direction.

Super Full Moon in Capricorn

Place	Date	Time
London	13 July	19:37
Sydney	14 July	04:37
Los Angeles	13 July	11:37
New York	13 July	14:37

This is such a powerful Full Moon! There's no real way of knowing exactly what will be going on in your life or the world when you read this, but one thing's for sure: if the situation is already tense, this is a week for us to tread very carefully, no matter what our Star sign or Rising sign, race, colour or creed! This Full Moon isn't an eclipse but it's placed so close to the eruptive planet Pluto that it might as well be. The issues you've been ignoring in the hope they'll go away are the very issues most likely to be stirred up by this Full Moon, so whatever you're angry about and have been trying to spiritually bypass – well, good luck with that! This Full Moon is a pot stirred, and evidently what we all need now (or it wouldn't be happening).

If you know that someone or something in your life has become toxic, you need to clear the air, detox and clean. That includes relationships, situations at work and even just your home if it's become really messy.

If pride has been holding you back or you've been acting purely from your ego, then again: watch out! This Full Moon could blow things up so that you have to come from the heart and leave your ego out of it.

There's good news, though: any crises that this Full Moon seemingly brings about (in truth, it's just the time for them to erupt) can bring healing, too.

✸ What This Lunation Means for You

To discover where the energy of this Full Moon is for you, find your Star sign or Rising sign here, see which House is involved, and then read A Quick Guide to the Houses (*see pages 15–16*): Aries – 10th House; Taurus – 9th House; Gemini – 8th House; Cancer – 7th House; Leo – 6th House; Virgo – 5th House; Libra – 4th House; Scorpio – 3rd House; Sagittarius – 2nd House; Capricorn – 1st House; Aquarius – 12th House; Pisces – 11th House.

✸ Detox Your Life

One of the best ways to work with the Full Moon energy this month is to detox your life. Consider cutting out any unhealthy foods or drinks, at the very least for the day of the Full Moon, better yet for the Full Moon phase (which lasts for about three days after the Full Moon first appears). Also, detox your house. Truly, the less clutter you have, the better your life will flow.

Full Moon Forgiveness and Release List

Given the power of this Full Moon, you'll be doing yourself a big favour if you work extra hard on releasing what's no longer good for you – and remember that forgiveness brings release. The good news is that, since the Full Moon is in the down-to-earth sign of Capricorn, which always faces facts, it's going to be easier than usual to be really honest about what to release – and about who you should forgive this month. Write it down below or on a separate sheet of paper, as you then need to burn it. I'll be holding a fire ceremony (for free) on Facebook (see moonmessages.com/fbevents).

I forgive/release:

_____

_____

_____

_____

_____

_____

⚸ Questions to Ask at This Full Moon

Are there any relationships or situations that I'm clinging on to for all the wrong reasons?

_____

_____

_____

_____

Where in my life is pride holding me back?

_____

_____

_____

_____

Where in my life do I need to transform, and what is the first step?

_____

_____

_____

_____

July Week 28

---

11 Monday ♐︎ ◯

---

12 Tuesday ♐︎♑︎ ◯

---

13 Wednesday ♑︎ ◯

Super Full Moon occurs at 21°Cp21
London   19:37
Los Angeles 11:37
New York   14:37

---

14 Thursday ♑︎♒︎ ◯

Super Full Moon occurs at 21°Cp21
Sydney   04:37

○ ♒   Friday 15

○ ♒ ♓   Saturday 16

○ ♓   Sunday 17

This Week

This Full Moon week could be up and down, with both easy
and challenging planetary alignments. The key to emerging
unscathed is to keep the lines of communication fully open.

July Week 29

18 Monday

19 Tuesday

20 Wednesday

What are you grateful for right now?

21 Thursday

◐ ♉   Friday **22**

◑ ♉♊   Saturday **23**

◑ ♊   Sunday **24**

This Week

We're now in the waning cycle of the Moon, which
is the period from Full Moon to New Moon, so
let it all go, let it fall away and... release.

New Moon in Leo

Place	Date	Time
London	28 July	18:54
Sydney	29 July	03:54
Los Angeles	28 July	10:54
New York	28 July	13:54

Leo is the showy sign of the zodiac; wherever you have Leo in your chart (and we all have all 12 signs in our chart), is where you like to show off, where you're creative and where you shine. This New Moon in Leo, though, is electric almost to the point of being dangerous! It's being aided and abetted by a clash between Mercury – the planet of the mind, language and words – and Uranus – the planet of chaos and electricity, radical change and turnarounds. In other words, the skies are on fire and we all need to tread carefully. It's going to be way too easy to say too much and regret it later. Leo is already a Fire sign, so adding this fire to the electrics of Uranus makes a volatile combination. The best way to handle it is to ground yourself and meditate.

This is also a very interesting New Moon in terms of making your wishes and setting your intentions. Don't be surprised if you put something out into the Universe and then change your mind, deciding you don't want it after all. My advice here would be to listen to your inner voice. Sometimes we seek things with our ego rather than our heart, and that never ends well!

☌ What This Lunation Means for You

To discover where the energy of this New Moon is for you, find your Star sign or Rising sign here, see which House is involved, and then read A Quick Guide to the Houses (see pages 15-16): Aries – 5th House; Taurus – 4th House; Gemini – 3rd House; Cancer – 2nd House; Leo – 1st House; Virgo – 12th House; Libra – 11th House; Scorpio – 10th House; Sagittarius – 9th House; Capricorn – 8th House; Aquarius – 7th House; Pisces – 6th House.

☌ Ground Yourself!

When the New Moon is as electric as this one, we're all going to need some grounding – when you consciously reconnect to the planet; when you bring yourself back down to earth if you've been feeling ungrounded or floaty. All you need do is walk barefoot on the ground. Note that, quite often, if we need grounding but do nothing about it, we tend to overeat. Eating is a very grounding process because it's so physical.

● New Moon Mantra ●

Om Namo Bhagavate Ramachandraya Namaha.

This mantra honours the Sun, which rules the sign of Leo. You can listen to it at moonologydiary.com.

New Moon Wishes and Intentions

My current biggest, most audacious goal, wish or intention at this New Moon is:

_____

Now turn it into an affirmation.

Write it here as if it has already happened:

_____

I commit to reciting this affirmation, with conviction, multiple times a day for the next month.

Sign here:

_____

Now add three micro-goals for this month that feed into your main goal:

_____

_____

_____

My other wishes, intentions and goals for this month, and action points I can take towards them, are:

1. My goal/wish/intention:

_____

The action I will take to make this happen:

_____

_____

2. My goal/wish/intention:

_____

The action I will take to make this happen:

_____

_____

3. My goal/wish/intention:

_____

The action I will take to make this happen:

_____

_____

Bring it home with a visualization ceremony.
Visit moonologydiary.com for a visualization audio meditation.

July Week 30

---

25 Monday

---

26 Tuesday

---

27 Wednesday

---

28 Thursday

New Moon occurs at 05°Le38
London   18:54
Los Angeles 10:54
New York   13:54

Friday **29**

New Moon occurs at 05°Le38
Sydney   03:54

Saturday **30**

Sunday **31**

This Week

The most important thing to do this week is to think about
how well – or not – you're communicating. Try not to
have knee-jerk reactions – the only secret is to *breathe*!

August

The month kicks off like a firecracker, with a meeting between fiery Mars and electric Uranus. These two are combustible when they get together, so if you're feeling like the lid is blowing off your life, that's probably why. Take it easy as the month begins, though not long afterwards Mars goes on to clash with Saturn as well! All in all, it's a pretty intense first week with tempers flaring, egos clashing and little time to relax.

The good news is that from 7 August onwards the vibe is much more laid-back and cooperative. Time to breathe! There's room for healing and even some passion. However, be aware that if you're trying to get something done, there could be a bit of going backwards and forwards, even some sudden reversals, due to a clash between the Sun and Uranus, the planet that loves to make turnarounds. Also, in the middle of the month a Sun–Saturn clash could put a few noses out of joint.

If you have a big subject that needs discussing, around 21–22 August there are some positive Mercury vibes – Mercury is the planet of communication so when he's in a good mood, better communication follows.

The month closes on a slightly jarring note as the planet Venus, which is all about love and abundance, clashes with

Saturn, which is all about limitations and restrictions. So if you feel like the milk of human kindness has dried up at the end of the month, don't panic: this too shall pass...

This month's Full Moon is in the sign of Aquarius and the New Moon is in the sign of Virgo. More about those as the month unfolds.

M	T	W	T	F	S	S
1	2	3	4	5 ◐	6	7
8	9	10	11	12 ○	13	14
15	16	17	18	19 ◑	20	21
22	23	24	25	26	27 ●	28
29	30	31				

~ Things to do this month ~

1. Turn your love life around.
2. Make a plan to improve your finances.
3. Believe in your own good luck.

August Week 31

1 Monday

Festivals of Lammas (northern hemisphere)
and Imbolc (southern hemisphere)

2 Tuesday

3 Wednesday

4 Thursday

Friday **5**

What are you grateful for right now?

☾ ♍ ♐ Saturday **6**

☾ ♐ Sunday **7**

This Week
There's a lot of potential for lovely things this week but you'll wreck it all instantly if you go at someone with your nostrils flared!

Full Moon in Aquarius

Place	Date	Time
London	12 August	02:35
Sydney	12 August	11:35
Los Angeles	11 August	18:35
New York	11 August	21:35

This Full Moon involves a clash between the Sun (ego) and retrograde Saturn (deconstruction), which is currently in Aquarius. The Full Moon always brings intensity, but this time there's going to be even more pressure than usual because Saturn is involved. It could be that someone is bossing you around, or maybe you're the one being heavy-handed. There could be rules being imposed on you that you're none too happy about. The best-case scenario is that previously laid-down rules are now finally being lifted.

To understand Saturn in Aquarius, let's talk in keywords. We're in a period of time when humanity (Aquarius represents humanity) has a lot of lessons to learn (Saturn teaches lessons). With a bit of luck, this lunation will see us all having evolved and learned lessons since this cycle started back in March 2020 – around the time the first coronavirus lockdown began. It's also about endings and releasing. It's slow and steady, and asks us to think about where we've come from and how far we've come.

On the plus side, it seems very likely that the emotional hysteria that quite often comes up at the time of the Full Moon will be dampened down by the presence of Saturn. Saturn isn't a planet that takes anything lightly, including histrionics.

If you know you need to quit someone or something, this is the Full Moon to cut ties. There will be less emotion involved, and more logic.

What This Lunation Means for You

To discover where the energy of this Full Moon is for you, find your Star sign or Rising sign here, see which House is involved, and then read A Quick Guide to the Houses (*see pages 15–16*): Aries – 11th House; Taurus – 10th House; Gemini – 9th House; Cancer – 8th House; Leo – 7th House; Virgo – 6th House; Libra – 5th House; Scorpio – 4th House; Sagittarius – 3rd House; Capricorn – 2nd House; Aquarius – 1st House; Pisces – 12th House.

A Release Ritual

If you work with angels, this is a great month to tune in to Archangel Azrael who helps us to handle our sadness and grief when we experience loss. Whatever else you do this Full Moon, make sure you draw up a list of whatever you know you need to leave behind – toxic relationships, a job you don't love, a living situation that's turned bad – and act on it! Then ask Archangel Azrael to help you process your emotions as you burn the list.

Full Moon Forgiveness and Release List

Every month is a good month to let go of stuff that's holding you back. We all have it – we start accumulating it from childhood. You may already know the benefits of ongoing release work; but if not, it really is never too late to start. The Aquarius Full Moon is an extra-special time for release work because Aquarius's energy is aloof and detached, making it easier to let things go. You can join me (for free) on Facebook where I'll be doing a fire ceremony (see moonmessages.com/fbevents). What are you releasing?

I forgive/release:

_____

_____

_____

_____

_____

_____

_____

⚹ Questions to Ask at This Full Moon

What am I clinging on to that I know is doing me no good?

_____

_____

.

_____

_____

_____

What can I do for the good of the planet?

_____

_____

_____

_____

How much am I loving my job? Or is it time to move on?

_____

_____

_____

_____

August Week 32

....

8 Monday ♐♑ ◗

....

9 Tuesday ♑ ◗

....

10 Wednesday ♑♒ ◗

....

11 Thursday ♒ ○

Full Moon occurs at 19°Aq21
Los Angeles 18:35
New York   21:35

....

○ ♒ ♓   Friday 12

Full Moon occurs at 19°Aq21
London   02:35
Sydney   11:35

○ ♓   Saturday 13

○ ♓ ♈   Sunday 14

This Week

The Full Moon could make this week feel quite challenging,
but if you make an extra effort with the release work,
you could feel quite transformed by mid-August.

August Week 33

---

15 Monday

---

16 Tuesday

---

17 Wednesday

---

18 Thursday

Friday 19

What are you grateful for right now?

 Saturday 20

Sunday 21

This Week

If there's someone you love or want to seduce, make a
date on 17 August – it's one of the most romantic nights
of the year. It's also great for socializing with friends.

New Moon in Virgo

Place	Date	Time
London	27 August	08:16
Sydney	27 August	17:16
Los Angeles	27 August	00:16
New York	27 August	03:16

This New Moon is the ideal time to gather your energy as we face towards the end of the year. It's in the sign of Virgo, the chaste and modest sign of the zodiac that's all about counting beans and being practical and systematic. Virgo is very good for organization and asks us to cross our T's and dot our I's. So, how are you doing? Does your life feel like it's moving in the right direction? Do you feel like your health goals are on track? If not, then harness the energies of this New Moon to get back on track.

Just before the New Moon, there's a clash between Venus, the planet of love and abundance, and erratic Uranus – and there's also a clash between the Sun, the Moon and Mars. All in all, life could feel rather tense! Things may feel like they're spinning out of control or that some people are just in the mood to pick a fight. After the New Moon, we get an alignment between loving Venus and stern Saturn which, in all truth, could go either way. If you're having big issues in an important relationship, personal or professional, matters could come to a head. If you're surrounded by people you love and who love you, things should feel more stable soon after the New Moon.

What This Lunation Means for You

To discover where the energy of this New Moon is for you, find your Star sign or Rising sign here, see which House is involved, and then read A Quick Guide to the Houses (*see pages 15–16*): Aries – 6th House; Taurus – 5th House; Gemini – 4th House; Cancer – 3rd House; Leo – 2nd House; Virgo – 1st House; Libra – 12th House; Scorpio – 11th House; Sagittarius – 10th House; Capricorn – 9th House; Aquarius – 8th House; Pisces – 7th House.

Get Your Finances Sorted

This New Moon might not be the easiest one of the year but it does offer a great opportunity to get our financial ducks in a row. If you have unopened bills, or you've been avoiding any other thankless financial tasks, such as checking your receipts for tax purposes, tackle them now. It's the perfect time to face financial fears and get financially organized.

● New Moon Mantra ●

Om Namo Bhagavate Buddha Devaya Namaha.

This mantra honours the planet Mercury, the sign that rules Virgo. You can listen to it at moonologydiary.com.

New Moon Wishes and Intentions

My current biggest, most audacious goal, wish or intention at this New Moon is:

_____

Now turn it into an affirmation.

Write it here as if it has already happened:

_____

I commit to reciting this affirmation, with conviction, multiple times a day for the next month.

Sign here:

_____

Now add three micro-goals for this month that feed into your main goal:

_____

_____

_____

My other wishes, intentions and goals for this month, and action points I can take towards them, are:

1. My goal/wish/intention:

_____

The action I will take to make this happen:

_____

_____

2. My goal/wish/intention:

_____

The action I will take to make this happen:

_____

_____

3. My goal/wish/intention:

_____

The action I will take to make this happen:

_____

_____

Bring it home with a visualization ceremony.
Visit moonologydiary.com for a visualization audio meditation.

August Week 34

....

22 Monday

....

23 Tuesday

....

24 Wednesday

....

25 Thursday

....

Friday 26

Saturday 27

New Moon occurs at 04°Vi03

London	08:16
Sydney	17:16
Los Angeles	00:16
New York	03:16

Sunday 28

This Week

The days in the lead-up to the New Moon this week are
an excellent time to convince someone of something,
or if you need some healing after a broken heart.

September

When you look at the astrology for September 2022, it seems quite innocuous. There are no eclipses, no big outer-planet sign changes and no big clashes. In fact, what you get this month is more or less endless ease. That might sound a bit hard to believe, but the fact is the astrology for September really is rather pleasant. So the best thing we can all do is take it easy. Cruise.

The month kicks off with a harmonious alignment between feisty Mars and lucky Jupiter, so go into whatever you're doing this month in the knowledge that you have the celestial forces on your side.

On 10 September, Mercury retrograde begins. This is a time when you want to review your life rather than pressing forwards with new plans. Remember that the most intense parts of any retrograde are the start and the end of the cycle, so wait a week or so after the cycle ends on 2 October to do things such as confirming travel plans, or buying a new car, a new computer or a new phone. In the meantime, while Mercury is retrograde, don't be surprised if you fall out with someone, an email goes astray, or you experience disruptions to technology, communications or travel plans.

This particular Mercury retrograde is in the sign of Libra, so you may have been rethinking at least one very important relationship in your life. By the middle of the month you should have digested all the information that's come your way over the past few weeks and be ready to take action.

M	T	W	T	F	S	S
			1	2	3 ◑	4
5	6	7	8	9	10 ○	11
12	13	14	15	16	17 ◐	18
19	20	21	22	23	24	25 ●
26	27	28	29	30		

~ Things to do this month ~

1. Go for it!
2. Make an important relationship decision.
3. Push your luck (but not too much).

Aug/Sept Week 35

29 Monday

....

30 Tuesday

....

31 Wednesday

....

1 Thursday

....

♏︎⚹♐︎   Friday 2

○♐︎   Saturday 3

What are you grateful for right now?

◐♐︎   Sunday 4

This Week

Probably the biggest danger this week is that
you could say too much too soon. Otherwise,
the skies are looking pretty positive.

Full Moon in Pisces

Place	Date	Time
London	10 September	10:59
Sydney	10 September	19:59
Los Angeles	10 September	02:59
New York	10 September	05:59

The Full Moon in Pisces can be a relatively mellow time. At this Full Moon, the Sun is in the opposite sign, Virgo, the most modest and chaste sign; Virgo counts the beans and takes care of duties and responsibilities. Pisces, on the other hand, is the sign of dreams and mysteries, swimming away to escape reality. So around this time of the year, there's usually a tug of war dividing your attention between all the things on your 'To Do' list and the fact that you'd probably like to be lying on a beach somewhere, sipping pina coladas (or is that just me?!).

This year, though, the Full Moon in Pisces is a bit different. It's being strongly influenced by a close alignment with the planet of change and craziness, Uranus, so even though there's the usual dreamy flavour to this Full Moon, if it's change you're dreaming of, then watch out: you could be about to get it!

Get a jump on this Full Moon by deciding where you want to make a radical change. Then tap into the Piscean energy by creating a vision board (*see below*), or just daydream about the big change you want to see. Sudden reversals and major turnarounds are highly likely at the moment.

The good news is that, even though the idea of big changes might sound a little bit worrying, the fact that the Full Moon is *harmonizing* with Uranus means any changes now are probably going to feel smooth and easy.

⚳ What This Lunation Means for You

To discover where the energy of this Full Moon is for you, find your Star sign or Rising sign here, see which House is involved, and then read A Quick Guide to the Houses (*see pages 15–16*): Aries – 12th House; Taurus – 11th House; Gemini – 10th House; Cancer – 9th House; Leo – 8th House; Virgo – 7th House; Libra – 6th House; Scorpio – 5th House; Sagittarius – 4th House; Capricorn – 3rd House; Aquarius – 2nd House; Pisces – 1st House.

⚳ Make a Vision Board

If you haven't already made a vision board this year, do it now. All you need are some old magazines, or access to the Internet and a printer. Think about what you want to manifest – for example, a holiday in the Bahamas. Research the Bahamas, print images you love and that represent what the Bahamas means to you, then make like a kid in primary school and stick them on a piece of cardboard. Put this vision board somewhere private where you can enjoy it and dream about it: dreams can come true, remember?

Full Moon Forgiveness and Release List

As well as being a great time to practise forgiveness, the Full Moon is ideal for releasing any resistance that's holding you back. Once you've done both, you'll be amazed how quickly life changes. This month's work is even easier because Pisces is such a forgiving sign, so tap into your compassion. Write down what you want to forgive and release, or use a separate sheet of paper, as you should ideally then burn your list. Join me (for free) on Facebook where I'll be doing a fire ceremony (see moonmessages.com/fbevents).

I forgive/release:

_____

_____

_____

_____

_____

_____

_____

⚸ Questions to Ask at This Full Moon

Have I been kidding myself about something, and, if so, what do I need to wake up to?

_____

_____

_____

_____

Where could I use a radical turnaround in my life?

_____

_____

_____

_____

Am I resisting forgiving someone that I really need to pardon, so I can move on? What's holding me back?

_____

_____

_____

_____

September Week 36

5 Monday ♐♑ ◐

6 Tuesday ♑ ◐

7 Wednesday ♑♒ ◯

8 Thursday ♒ ◯

○ ♒ ♓   Friday **9**

───────────────────────────────

○ ♓   Saturday **10**

Full Moon occurs at 17°Pi41
London   10:59
Sydney   19:59
Los Angeles   02:59
New York   05:59
Mercury goes retrograde (until 2 October).

───────────────────────────────

○ ♓ ♈   Sunday **11**

───────────────────────────────

This Week

That little trickster of the zodiac, Mercury, begins his
latest retrograde cycle on 10 September. This time
around, Mercury is retrograde in the signs of Libra
and Virgo. Relationship confusion could arise.

September Week 37

12 Monday

....

13 Tuesday

....

14 Wednesday

....

15 Thursday

....

 Friday 16

 Saturday 17

What are you grateful for right now?

♑ Ⅱ ♋ Sunday 18

This Week

This week sees a clash between the two lovers
of the zodiac, Venus and Mars. Unexpectedly,
when these two clash what you get is a nice
vive la différence frisson rather than anything else.

New Moon in Libra

Place	Date	Time
London	25 September	22:54
Sydney	26 September	07:54
Los Angeles	25 September	14:54
New York	25 September	17:54

This New Moon is in the rather lovely sign of Libra. Life goes in cycles, and right now there should be enough pleasant things happening for you to feel as though life isn't always tough.

If you're single, this is most certainly the month to draw a line under the past. If you're pining after your ex, try to set that aside and open up your heart to the idea of new love with someone better suited to you. I'm not saying you can't reunite with your ex; I'm just saying it's good to be open to whatever the Universe has in mind for you. If you're already attached, tap into this New Moon to refresh the romance and love that you have. All relationships need work, so if you only do the work once a year, do it around the time of the New Moon in Libra.

In fact, the stage is doubly set for romance at the moment. The first planetary alignment after this New Moon is between Venus and Pluto. Something will be in the air, that's for sure! New loves will be starting, and existing relationships will be blossoming. Good vibes also apply to family and professional relationships.

☓ What This Lunation Means for You

To discover where the energy of this New Moon is for you, find your Star sign or Rising sign here, see which House is involved, and then read A Quick Guide to the Houses (*see pages 15–16*): Aries – 7th House; Taurus – 6th House; Gemini – 5th House; Cancer – 4th House; Leo – 3rd House; Virgo – 2nd House; Libra – 1st House; Scorpio – 12th House; Sagittarius – 11th House; Capricorn – 10th House; Aquarius – 9th House; Pisces – 8th House.

☓ Honour Lakshmi

A beautiful thing to do this New Moon is to create a small altar to Lakshmi, the Hindu goddess of love and abundance. Put a picture of her at the centre and add items representing the elements – earth (perhaps place a crystal), fire (a candle), air (a bell) and water (in a pretty tumbler). Light the candle and talk to Lakshmi whenever you spend time at your altar between the New and Full Moons.

● New Moon Mantra ●

Om Namo Bhagavate Para Surama Ya Namaha.

This mantra honours Venus, the planet that rules the sign of Libra. You can listen to it at moonologydiary.com.

New Moon Wishes and Intentions

My current biggest, most audacious goal, wish or intention at this New Moon is:

_____

Now turn it into an affirmation.

Write it here as if it has already happened:

_____

I commit to reciting this affirmation, with conviction, multiple times a day for the next month.

Sign here:

_____

Now add three micro-goals for this month that feed into your main goal:

_____

_____

_____

My other wishes, intentions and goals for this month, and action points I can take towards them, are:

1. My goal/wish/intention:

_____

The action I will take to make this happen:

_____

_____

2. My goal/wish/intention:

_____

The action I will take to make this happen:

_____

_____

3. My goal/wish/intention:

_____

The action I will take to make this happen:

_____

_____

Bring it home with a visualization ceremony.
Visit moonologydiary.com for a visualization audio meditation.

September Week 38

19 Monday

20 Tuesday

21 Wednesday

22 Thursday

Friday 23

Autumn Equinox/Mabon (northern hemisphere) and
Spring Equinox/Ostara (southern hemisphere)

Saturday 24

Sunday 25

New Moon occurs at 02°Li48
London   22:54
Los Angeles 14:54
New York   17:54

This Week

This week brings a lovely link between Venus, the planet
of love, and Neptune, the planet of soul mates. It really is
the right time to turn your thoughts and heart to love.

September Week 39

....

26 Monday
New Moon occurs at 02°Li48
Sydney 07:54

....

27 Tuesday

....

28 Wednesday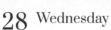

....

29 Thursday

....

◗ ♏︎→♐︎   Friday 30

◗ ♐︎   Saturday 1

◖ ♐︎♑︎   Sunday 2

Mercury retrograde ends.

This Week

We're now in the waxing cycle of the Moon,
the most important time for taking inspired
action around your New Moon wishes.

October

October is a big month! The first thing to know is that on 2 October Mercury retrograde ends. This may have been a frustrating retrograde for some, especially as it was in the sign of pedantic Virgo, but if you used the time wisely, it may have been a wonderful chance to cross some T's and dot some I's. Two of the major outer planets, Pluto and Saturn, also end their retrograde cycles this month. Pluto and Saturn are each very challenging, and when they go retrograde we get a second chance to prove ourselves. Once they're 'going forwards' again, though, we can expect a whole new set of challenges!

There's also a New Moon eclipse this month – in the sign of Scorpio. Eclipses are enhancers, and they often make good things better, but if you're living negatively, it can be a time when you feel forced to make changes, whether you're ready for them or not. That said, this eclipse is in the same place as the love planet Venus, which augurs well.

Finally, we see the big planet of good luck and good times, Jupiter, moving back into Pisces for one last hurrah before departing for at least a decade. That means we're all about to get one last shot of good luck in our birth chart, and therefore our lives. To find out where this luck is for you, take a look at 'What This Lunation Means for You' for the New Moon in Pisces (*see page 63*). Jupiter is now in the same part of your chart.

M	T	W	T	F	S	S
					1	2
3 ◗	4	5	6	7	8	9 ○
10	11	12	13	14	15	16
17 ◖	18	19	20	21	22	23
24	25 ●	26	27	28	29	30
31						

~ Things to do this month ~

1. Gather information to make a decision.
2. Let someone or something go.
3. Make a change in your life.

Full Moon in Aries

Place	Date	Time
London	9 October	21:54
Sydney	10 October	07:54
Los Angeles	9 October	13:54
New York	9 October	16:54

The first thing to note about this Full Moon is that it's taking place in Aries, which is the first sign of the zodiac. This means that, even though we're getting closer to the end of the year, it's a good time to recommit to your Moon practice. Decide now that you'll set aside time for it at every New or Full Moon. Hopefully by now you'll have seen the power of working with the lunar cycle. Note, however, that many people get so excited about making New Moon wishes that they forget their Full Moon work – but Full Moon releasing is at least as important as the New Moon intentions you set.

I've heard it explained like this: the Divine knows what you want. We, too, are Divine, so making wishes at New Moon is great because it gives us clarity about what we want while the Divine part of us, our soul, can start to make that happen. However, sometimes what we want isn't what's best for us. That's where the Full Moon comes in. If something hasn't turned out well and we surrender it to that part of us that's Divine, it's like saying, 'Here, you handle this. I don't have all the answers.' After all, while we may be Divine, we're also human.

Think about all this now as this Full Moon harmonizes with Venus, Saturn and then Mars, which means the energies are very supportive. This Full Moon is also taking place as the Sun moves near the planet of love and abundance, Venus, and the Moon is near the planetoid of healing, Chiron. All in all, that gives a rather lovely energy to this lunation.

✸ What This Lunation Means for You

To discover where the energy of this Full Moon is for you, find your Star sign or Rising sign here, see which House is involved, and then read A Quick Guide to the Houses (*see pages 15–16*): Aries – 1st House; Taurus – 12th House; Gemini – 11th House; Cancer – 10th House; Leo – 9th House; Virgo – 8th House; Libra – 7th House; Scorpio – 6th House; Sagittarius – 5th House; Capricorn – 4th House; Aquarius – 3rd House; Pisces – 2nd House.

✸ Call on an Angel

Tap into this lovely, healing Full Moon by calling on Archangel Raphael, the supreme healer of the angelic realm – his name means 'God heals' or 'He who heals' in Hebrew. Whether you need healing, or it's for someone you know and love, ask Raphael for help. Place a picture of him on your home altar, if you have one. It's said that Raphael often comes to us in our dreams so talk to him before you turn off your bedside light.

Full Moon Forgiveness and Release List

Even though it's only October, it's a good time to revive your Full Moon practices or go back to basics. List what you want to forgive and release; ask what's holding you back. It might be a childhood memory or someone in your current life – you don't need to release them from your life, but you might pay less attention to their opinion! You can tell who to forgive if thinking about them gives you a slight charge – it'll vanish once they're forgiven. Ideally, now burn your list – join me (for free) on Facebook for a fire ceremony (see moonmessages. com/fbevents).

I forgive/release:

_____

_____

_____

_____

_____

_____

✳ Questions to Ask at This Full Moon

What can I focus on in my life that shows me how lucky I am?

_____

_____

_____

_____

How can I commit to 12 months of working with the Full Moon?

_____

_____

_____

_____

What in my life needs healing, and what would that healing look like?

_____

_____

_____

_____

October Week 40

3 Monday

What are you grateful for right now?

4 Tuesday

5 Wednesday

6 Thursday

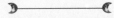

◐ ♓   Friday 7

◐ ♓ ♈   Saturday 8

○ ♈   Sunday 9

Full Moon occurs at 16°Ar32
London   21:54
Los Angeles   13:54
New York   16:54

This Week

Pluto, the planet of transformation, ends its latest retrograde cycle this week. That takes the pressure off us where we've been trying so hard to make changes, but it also unleashes a whole new cycle of transformation.

October Week 41

---

10 Monday

Full Moon occurs at 16°Ar32
Sydney   07:54

---

11 Tuesday

---

12 Wednesday

---

13 Thursday

Week 41 October

 Friday 14

Saturday 15

Sunday 16

This Week

Thanks to a lovely link between the planet of love and abundance, Venus, and the planet of commitments and contracts, Saturn, this is a great week to make a commitment, be that a love thing or a business contract.

October Week 42

17 Monday

What are you grateful for right now?

18 Tuesday

19 Wednesday

20 Thursday

Friday 21

Saturday 22

Sunday 23

This Week

Every now and then the Universe sends a reminder of the difference between love and obsession. We're getting one of those reminders this week – do you need it? It could also be a reminder not to be obsessed with money.

New Moon Eclipse
in Scorpio

Place	Date	Time
London	25 October	11:48
Sydney	25 October	21:48
Los Angeles	25 October	03:48
New York	25 October	06:48

If you're up for a bit of excitement and some change in your life, then this week is the one for you. New Moon eclipses are when portals open up to another life. While a Full Moon eclipse tends to be more about climaxes and endings, a New Moon eclipse is like a super-powered chance to make some massive changes in your life.

The wonderful thing about this eclipse is that it's taking place close to Venus, the planet of love and abundance. There's always an element of uncertainty about an eclipse, though, so if you've wandered far from the path that's best for you, now could be the time when you get unceremoniously shunted back onto the track you signed up for before you incarnated on earth.

If you've been doing the right thing when it comes to love and abundance in your life, what happens now could propel you in a wonderful new direction. What's more, just after the New Moon there's a brilliant alignment between Mercury, the planet of communication, and Mars, the planet of action, which means you have a chance to influence your outcomes with some determined language – so get talking!

✳ What This Lunation Means for You

To discover where the energy of this New Moon is for you, find your Star sign or Rising sign here, see which House is involved, and then read A Quick Guide to the Houses (*see pages 15–16*): Aries – 8th House; Taurus – 7th House; Gemini – 6th House; Cancer – 5th House; Leo – 4th House; Virgo – 3rd House; Libra – 2nd House; Scorpio – 1st House; Sagittarius – 12th House; Capricorn – 11th House; Aquarius – 10th House; Pisces – 9th House.

✳ Work on your Venus issues

The planet of love and abundance is very much involved in this exciting New Moon eclipse, so use the opportunity to sort out problems with money or your relationship, and make sure they feature when you set your New Moon intentions.

● New Moon Mantra ●

Om Krum Krutantakaya Namaha.

This mantra honours the traditional ruler of Scorpio, the planet Pluto. You can listen to it at moonologydiary.com.

New Moon Wishes and Intentions

My current biggest, most audacious goal, wish or intention at this New Moon is:

_____

Now turn it into an affirmation.

Write it here as if it has already happened:

_____

I commit to reciting this affirmation, with conviction, multiple times a day for the next month.

Sign here:

_____

Now add three micro-goals for this month that feed into your main goal:

_____

_____

_____

My other wishes, intentions and goals for this month, and action points I can take towards them, are:

1. My goal/wish/intention:

_____

The action I will take to make this happen:

_____

_____

2. My goal/wish/intention:

_____

The action I will take to make this happen:

_____

_____

3. My goal/wish/intention:

_____

The action I will take to make this happen:

_____

_____

Bring it home with a visualization ceremony.
Visit moonologydiary.com for a visualization audio meditation.

October Week 43

....

24 Monday

♎

....

25 Tuesday

♎ ♏

New Moon eclipse occurs at 02°Sc00

London   11:48
Sydney   21:48
Los Angeles 03:48
New York   06:48

....

26 Wednesday

♏

....

27 Thursday

♏ ♐

....

 ♐

Friday **28**

♐♑

Saturday **29**

♑

Sunday **30**

This Week

This week is a big one, astrologically. Not only is there the New Moon eclipse in the sign of Scorpio, but the lucky planet, Jupiter, is retrograde and moves out of Aries into Pisces, plus Mars goes retrograde.

November

As November begins, we're still well and truly in the eclipse season. That means now is a good time to be working hard on your dreams Moonology-style, i.e. turning your goals into affirmations that you recite, and visualizing and meditating on them. However, it also means taking inspired action. So, what practical steps can you take towards making your dreams real as November dawns? It's a super-intense time energy-wise, so make sure you do your best manifesting, particularly in the lead-up to the Full Moon on 8 November.

The rest of the month should be relatively smooth sailing. Once we've moved through the Full Moon eclipse and into the waning cycle, we're out of the eclipse season. If you're sensitive to energy and you pay attention, you'll see just how different and less intense life feels after the Full Moon eclipse has passed.

The energies for the rest of the month are calm and positive. The only caution is a second clash between Mars retrograde and Neptune on 19 November. There could be some confusing upsets around this time, so don't wade into any arguments if you can help it! The fact that Mars is retrograde is also something to be aware of more generally this month. Remember, Mars is the planet of action, so when it's retrograde it can be hard to push forward with plans. Try to consolidate at this time, rather than pushing ahead. Also see if you can put an end to an ongoing argument this month and make peace with someone.

M	T	W	T	F	S	S
	1	2	3	4	5	6
7	8	9	10	11	12	13
14	15	16	17	18	19	20
21	22	23	24	25	26	27
28	29	30				

~ Things to do this month ~

1. Step up your affirmation practice.
2. Turn the corner financially.
3. Hold your horses.

Oct/Nov Week 44

31 Monday

Festivals of Samhain (northern hemisphere) and Beltane (southern hemisphere)

1 Tuesday

What are you grateful for right now?

2 Wednesday

3 Thursday

Week 44 November

○♓♈ **Friday 4**

○♈ **Saturday 5**

○♈ **Sunday 6**

This Week

It's the last week before the Full Moon eclipse, so whatever it is you're manifesting, go hard at it! Turn your wishes into affirmations, visualize your dreams and focus on what you want (not on what you don't want).

Full Moon Eclipse
in Taurus

Place	Date	Time
London	8 November	11:02
Sydney	8 November	22:02
Los Angeles	8 November	03:02
New York	8 November	06:02

Full Moon eclipses are always intense, but this one promises to be all the more so. For one thing, it's taking place in the sign of Taurus, which is associated with money, so it's a good time to think about your finances and make some changes where cash is concerned. If you know you've been doubting yourself or selling yourself short financially, this is the eclipse to tap into to consciously create a better outcome for yourself.

However, that's not the only reason why this is an amazing, potentially electric eclipse – it's also taking place near the planet of radical change and sudden turnarounds, Uranus. The respective positions of the Full Moon at the time of the eclipse and the planet Uranus create a scenario that astrologers call partile, which means they're on exactly the same degree of the zodiac. That means it's time to hang on to your hats! Sudden changes are possible any time now.

The secret with all Full Moon eclipses, and in particular with one like this, is to let go of what no longer serves you. If you're clinging on to someone or something that you know is toxic in your life but that you're continuing with (most likely for all the wrong reasons), take a hint from the skies and let them or it go before the eclipse arrives. Releasing what no longer serves you voluntarily is much easier than having the eclipse unceremoniously rip it away.

⅏ What This Lunation Means for You

To discover where the energy of this Full Moon is for you, find your Star sign or Rising sign here, see which House is involved, and then read A Quick Guide to the Houses (*see pages 15–16*): Aries – 2nd House; Taurus – 1st House; Gemini – 12th House; Cancer – 11th House; Leo – 10th House; Virgo – 9th House; Libra – 8th House; Scorpio – 7th House; Sagittarius – 6th House; Capricorn – 5th House; Aquarius – 4th House; Pisces – 3rd House.

⅏ Automatic Writing

Automatic writing is a way to let your Higher Self speak out. At the top of a blank sheet of paper write: 'What did I come to this Earth to achieve?' Now take a deep breath and allow the answer to flow; just let your pen move. Even if you think you're writing the words yourself, allow for the possibility that you're tapping into your Higher Self and being guided with intuition and teaching.

Full Moon Forgiveness and Release List

Every Full Moon is a good time to forgive, let go and turn a corner, and a Full Moon eclipse is all that times 20! You may have bought this diary to use the celestial energies to better your life or to manifest something. Well, there's nothing more important when manifesting than emptying out all your negativity, so use this eclipse to banish any toxic emotions. List what you want to release and forgive, using a separate sheet if you don't want to burn this page. Join me (for free) on Facebook, where I'll be doing a fire ceremony (see moonmessages.com/fbevents).

I forgive/release:

_____

_____

_____

_____

_____

_____

✳ Questions to Ask at This Full Moon

Where have I been too controlling? How can I release my grip?

_____

_____

_____

_____

Where in my life do I need a radical turnaround? What do I need to know to create that?

_____

_____

_____

_____

Which toxic emotions am I willing to release, knowing this will help me?

_____

_____

_____

_____

November Week 45

7 Monday

8 Tuesday

Full Moon eclipse occurs at 10°Ta01
London   11:02
Sydney   22:02
Los Angeles   03:02
New York   06:02

9 Wednesday

10 Thursday

◑ ♊   Friday 11

◑ ♊ ♋   Saturday 12

◑ ♋   Sunday 13

This Week

This week brings the Full Moon eclipse in the sign
of Taurus. Make sure you tap into it – eclipses
are so powerful! I'll be doing a Facebook Live at
facebook.com/YasminBoland so please join me. It's also
a perfect time for a ceremony to release money worries.

November Week 46

---

14 Monday

---

15 Tuesday

---

16 Wednesday

What are you grateful for right now?

---

17 Thursday

Week 46 November

Friday 18

Saturday 19

Sunday 20

This Week

The skies this week are generally extremely positive. Take it as easy as you can, and if there's a spiritual practice that isn't working for you, give it a rest.

New Moon in Sagittarius

Place	Date	Time
London	23 November	22:57
Sydney	24 November	09:57
Los Angeles	23 November	14:57
New York	23 November	17:57

This week's New Moon takes place in Sagittarius, the sign ruled by the planet of good luck and good times, Jupiter. Jupiter has been retrograde for the past few months, but this week we get the Sagittarius New Moon just before the end of Jupiter retrograde. In other words, if you've been feeling trapped, that your luck isn't flowing as you want it to, as though you need an adventure or that you want to see the bigger picture of where you are in life, then this New Moon will help you. It'll certainly broaden all our horizons.

Note that this is the first lunation after the eclipse season. We won't get another series of eclipses for around six months, so if the past month or so has been a little bit turbulent, you can now rest safe in the knowledge that life is going to settle down a little for a while.

There are also some healing alignments taking place after this New Moon, so if there has been hurt in your life, the healing can take place now. Love and communication are the two keys to healing, at the moment. This is because the planet of communication, Mercury, and the planet of love, Venus, are both making harmonious connections with the healing planetoid, Chiron. Healing of all kinds is possible now.

丰 What This Lunation Means for You

To discover where the energy of this New Moon is for you, find your Star sign or Rising sign here, see which House is involved, and then read A Quick Guide to the Houses (*see pages 15–16*): Aries – 9th House; Taurus – 8th House; Gemini – 7th House; Cancer – 6th House; Leo – 5th House; Virgo – 4th House; Libra – 3rd House; Scorpio – 2nd House; Sagittarius – 1st House; Capricorn – 12th House; Aquarius – 11th House; Pisces – 10th House.

丰 Where Do You Want to Go?

A fun thing to do each time there's a New Moon in Sagittarius is make a list of where in the world you'd like to travel. As a first step towards realizing those plans, print out a world map and mark your desired destinations. Then either burn the list and map, or put them somewhere you'll see them all the time to keep your dreams alive.

● New Moon Mantra ●

Om Namo Bhagavate Vamana Devaya Namaha.

This mantra honours the planet Jupiter, which rules the sign of Sagittarius. You can listen to it at moonologydiary.com.

New Moon Wishes and Intentions

My current biggest, most audacious goal, wish or intention at this New Moon is:

_____

Now turn it into an affirmation.

Write it here as if it has already happened:

_____

I commit to reciting this affirmation, with conviction, multiple times a day for the next month.

Sign here:

_____

Now add three micro-goals for this month that feed into your main goal:

_____

_____

_____

My other wishes, intentions and goals for this month, and action points I can take towards them, are:

1. My goal/wish/intention:

_____

The action I will take to make this happen:

_____

_____

2. My goal/wish/intention:

_____

The action I will take to make this happen:

_____

_____

3. My goal/wish/intention:

_____

The action I will take to make this happen:

_____

_____

Bring it home with a visualization ceremony.
Visit moonologydiary.com for a visualization audio meditation.

November Week 47

....

21 Monday

....

22 Tuesday

....

23 Wednesday
New Moon occurs at 01°Sg37
London   22:57
Los Angeles   14:57
New York   17:57

....

24 Thursday
New Moon occurs at 01°Sg37
Sydney   09:57

....

Friday **25**

Saturday **26**

Sunday **27**

This Week

The planet of good luck, Jupiter, ends it retrograde cycle this week, so more luck will flow in whichever part of your chart Jupiter is in – check 'What This Lunation Means for You' for the New Moon in Pisces (*see page 63*).

December

Let's talk a little more about the planet Jupiter. In some ways, it should be everybody's favourite planet. After all, it's the planet of good luck, good fortune, good times and healing – pretty much all things good. I've even heard it said by one of the most respected astrologers in the world, Robert Hand, that there's no such thing as a bad Jupiter transit. So is Jupiter the answer to everybody's problems? In a way, yes.

The reason for mentioning Jupiter now is that it's making a rare change of sign. If you've been using the diary all year, you'll know that, back in May, Jupiter moved into the sign of Aries. Then, while going retrograde in October, it slipped back into the sign of Pisces for one last sojourn. Jupiter in Pisces has hopefully helped all of us to be more in touch with our spiritual side. Jupiter in Pisces only happens once every 12 years, and as of this month, it's done!

Now, Jupiter is moving back into the sign of Aries – back into the first sign of the zodiac and starting a whole new 12-year cycle. So, this month, commit to working with Jupiter (*see page 245*). Think about luck. The way to see whether you're lucky is to think about what blessings you have in your life. It's very easy to think, 'Oh, I never win anything,

I'm not lucky,' but there's more to luck than winning prizes. Take a moment this month to connect with where you *are* blessed. As my teacher in India, Sri Sakthi Narayani Amma, says, 'The secret is to know you are blessed, and live your life within that knowing.' Wise words indeed.

M	T	W	T	F	S	S
			1	2	3	4
5	6	7	8 ○	9	10	11
12	13	14	15	16 ◑	17	18
19	20	21	22	23 ●	24	25
26	27	28	29	30 ◐	31	

~ Things to do this month ~

1. Commit to working with Jupiter.
2. Review your year.
3. Practise gratitude.

Nov/Dec Week 48

28 Monday

29 Tuesday

30 Wednesday

What are you grateful for right now?

1 Thursday

◐ ⚹ ♑   Friday 2

◐ ♑   Saturday 3

◐ ♑ ♉   Sunday 4

This Week

There's quite a lot of confusion in the air this week as
the planet of deception, Neptune, is triggered twice.
The good news is that despite this, commitments
and contracts made this week are likely to stick.

Full Moon in Gemini

Place	Date	Time
London	8 December	04:08
Sydney	8 December	15:08
Los Angeles	7 December	20:08
New York	7 December	23:08

We can expect the energies of this last Full Moon of 2022 to be quite unusual, to say the least! It's taking place in the sign of Gemini, the sign of conversation, online comments, thoughts, and anything else to do with communication, so a Full Moon in Gemini may be a time where angry words are spoken, heated comments are exchanged and communication generally gets emotional.

The difference is that this year the Full Moon in Gemini is taking place smack bang on Mars, the planet of anger, which happens to be retrograde. One of the best ways to use this lunation is to see how much better life is when you don't lose your temper! Mars retrograde is a time when we all can learn to hold fire. Can you keep your cool, even when people are practically provoking you? That's the test from this Full Moon.

The good news is that the first alignment the Sun makes after the Full Moon is a harmonious one, with the planet

Saturn. So, if you can keep your own counsel at Full Moon, life should calm down substantially just a few days later. If all else fails, remember it's the season of goodwill, and just be nice! This Full Moon is also a perfect time for extra-deep forgiveness as you look back over the year and consider what to release that didn't work out, and who you need to forgive, including yourself.

✳ What This Lunation Means for You

To discover where the energy of this Full Moon is for you, find your Star sign or Rising sign here, see which House is involved, and then read A Quick Guide to the Houses (*see pages 15–16*): Aries – 3rd House; Taurus – 2nd House; Gemini – 1st House; Cancer – 12th House; Leo – 11th House; Virgo – 10th House; Libra – 9th House; Scorpio – 8th House; Sagittarius – 7th House; Capricorn – 6th House; Aquarius – 5th House; Pisces – 4th House.

✳ Let Go of 2022

I hope that 2022 has been a brilliant year for you. However, if there have been tough times, now is the time to let them go. The last Full Moon of the year is taking place in the sign of Gemini, which rules our minds. So soothe any troubled thoughts from this year by blessing the situation in question and anyone involved in it, and by forgiving everyone, including yourself. Offer up to the Divine any situations still not yet working the way you'd like them to, using these three simple Sanskrit words: 'Om Namo Narayani', which means 'I surrender to the Divine.' Let the Divine take care of everything.

Full Moon Forgiveness and Release List

This could be the most important Full Moon forgiveness-and-release ceremony you do all year, so make sure that 1) You do it and 2) You do it from the heart. Write down what didn't work out for you in 2022 that you're now letting go of – and really go into detail, taking at least 15 minutes – and then? Burn that list! (Use a separate sheet of paper if you don't want to burn this page.) You can join me (for free) on Facebook where I will be doing a fire ceremony (see moonmessages. com/fbevents).

Goodbye 2022. Thank you. I forgive and release the following:

_____

_____

_____

_____

_____

_____

_____

ⵣ Questions to Ask at This Full Moon

If negative thoughts are my enemy, what can I focus on in my life that's positive?

_____

_____

_____

_____

Which upset am I ready to move on from? How would I feel if I healed this upset? Is there someone I need to reach out to?

_____

_____

_____

How might releasing upsets from 2022 make 2023 a better year for me?

_____

_____

_____

_____

December Week 49

5 Monday ♉◐

....

6 Tuesday ♉♊○

....

7 Wednesday ♊○

Full Moon occurs at l6°Ge0l
Los Angeles   20:08
New York   23:08

....

8 Thursday ♊○

Full Moon occurs at l6°Ge0l
London   04:08
Sydney   l5:08

....

○ I ♋   Friday 9

○ ♋   Saturday 10

○ ♋ ♌   Sunday 11

This Week

The planet Jupiter is being triggered twice this week.
That means it's going to be easy to say too much, so
talk carefully. It's also going to be easy to smother
someone with a bit too much love. Lucky them!

December Week 50

12 Monday ♌︎○

13 Tuesday ♌︎○

14 Wednesday ♌︎♍︎○

15 Thursday ♍︎◑

 Friday 16

What are you grateful for right now?

 Saturday 17

♎ Sunday 18

This Week

If you need to have a big, important conversation, leave
it until the end of the week, when the tricky alignments
happening at the start of it will have passed.

Super New Moon in Capricorn

Place	Date	Time
London	23 December	10:16
Sydney	23 December	21:16
Los Angeles	23 December	02:16
New York	23 December	05:16

So we're approaching the last New Moon of the year, and I think you could say it's a bit of a doozy! At the time of the New Moon, there's what astrologers call a stellium, or cluster, of planets in Capricorn: we have the Sun, the Moon, Mercury, Venus and Pluto. That's a ton of Capricorn energy!

This stellium works really well with the season. Even though it's the end of the year and many people will be celebrating Christmas, Hanukkah or just the end of the year, we also should be mindful that a new year is about to begin and start thinking about our intentions for the year ahead.

If you do only one New Moon wishing ritual this year, make it this month! Sending out wishes for the year ahead, setting intentions, tapping into the New Moon – which is so powerful in Capricorn - and aligning with the Mercury-Venus-Neptune energies makes this the perfect time to devise an imaginative strategy, including ways to enjoy abundance and romance in 2023.

What This Lunation Means for You

To discover where the energy of this New Moon is for you, find your Star sign or Rising sign here, see which House is involved, and then read A Quick Guide to the Houses (*see pages 15–16*): Aries - 10th House; Taurus - 9th House; Gemini - 8th House; Cancer - 7th House; Leo - 6th House; Virgo - 5th House; Libra - 4th House; Scorpio - 3rd House; Sagittarius - 2nd House; Capricorn - 1st House; Aquarius - 12th House; Pisces - 11th House.

Commit to Jupiter

Let's go large and make a 12-year commitment! The planet of good luck and expansion, Jupiter, has just moved back into the first sign of the zodiac, Aries, which marks the start of a new 12-year Jupiter cycle. Take a look at 'What This Lunation Means for You' for the New Moon in Aries (*see page 81*) as Jupiter is bringing goodness to the same House. Look at how you can expand in that part of your life, and count your blessings too.

● New Moon Mantra ●

Om Namo Bhagavate Kurma Devaya Namaha.

This chant honours Saturn, which rules the sign of Capricorn. You can listen to it at moonologydiary.com.

New Moon Wishes and Intentions

How did I do with my biggest, most audacious goals, wishes and intentions of 2022?

_____

_____

_____

_____

_____

What aspects of those intentions do I need to take with me into 2023?

_____

_____

_____

_____

_____

What have I been most grateful for in 2022?

_____

_____

_____

_____

_____

_____

_____

What five life goals am I committing to in 2023?

1. _____

2. _____

3. _____

4. _____

5. _____

Bring it home with a visualization ceremony.
Visit moonologydiary.com for a visualization audio meditation.

December Week 51

19 Monday

....

20 Tuesday

....

21 Wednesday

Winter Solstice/Yule (northern hemisphere);
Summer Solstice/Litha (southern hemisphere)

....

22 Thursday ♐ ●

....

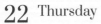

Friday **23**

Super New Moon occurs at 01°Cp32
London   10:16
Sydney   21:16
Los Angeles 02:16
New York   05:16

Saturday **24**

Sunday **25**

This Week

As much as this time of the year is about fun and celebration, it's also about being grateful for whatever has happened in the past year and dreaming of what you'd like to happen in the year ahead. This week's expansive, dreamy and change-making astrology supports that.

December Week 52

....

26 Monday

....

27 Tuesday

....

28 Wednesday

....

29 Thursday

Mercury goes retrograde (until 18 January 2023).
....

☽♈ Friday **30**

What are you grateful for right now?

● ♈♉ Saturday **31**

○ ♉ Sunday **1**

This Week
Mercury goes retrograde this week, so it's a perfect time to review the year and see which goals you didn't achieve and that you can try harder with next year.

January 2023 Week 1

2 Monday

3 Tuesday

4 Wednesday

5 Thursday

○♋   Friday **6**

Full Moon occurs at 16°Cn22
London   23:07
Los Angeles   15:07
New York   18:07

○♋   Saturday **7**

Full Moon occurs at 16°Cn22
Sydney   10:07

○♋♌   Sunday **8**

This Week

The first week of 2023 kicks off with Mercury
being retrograde, a Full Moon and a lovely link
between Venus and Jupiter that could be as
romantic as it is abundant. Expect good things!

JANUARY

M	T	W	T	F	S	S
						1
2	3	4	5	6	7	8
9	10	11	12	13	14	15
16	17	18	19	20	21	22
23	24	25	26	27	28	29
30	31					

FEBRUARY

M	T	W	T	F	S	S
	1	2	3	4	5	
6	7	8	9	10	11	12
13	14	15	16	17	18	19
20	21	22	23	24	25	26
27	28					

MARCH

M	T	W	T	F	S	S
	1	2	3	4	5	
6	7	8	9	10	11	12
13	14	15	16	17	18	19
20	21	22	23	24	25	26
27	28	29	30	31		

APRIL

M	T	W	T	F	S	S
				1	2	
3	4	5	6	7	8	9
10	11	12	13	14	15	16
17	18	19	20	21	22	23
24	25	26	27	28	29	30

MAY

M	T	W	T	F	S	S
1	2	3	4	5	6	7
8	9	10	11	12	13	14
15	16	17	18	19	20	21
22	23	24	25	26	27	28
29	30	31				

JUNE

M	T	W	T	F	S	S
		1	2	3	4	
5	6	7	8	9	10	11
12	13	14	15	16	17	18
19	20	21	22	23	24	25
26	27	28	29	30		

JULY

M	T	W	T	F	S	S
					1	2
3	4	5	6	7	8	9
10	11	12	13	14	15	16
17	18	19	20	21	22	23
24	25	26	27	28	29	30
31						

AUGUST

M	T	W	T	F	S	S
1	2	3	4	5	6	
7	8	9	10	11	12	13
14	15	16	17	18	19	20
21	22	23	24	25	26	27
28	29	30	31			

SEPTEMBER

M	T	W	T	F	S	S
				1	2	3
4	5	6	7	8	9	10
11	12	13	14	15	16	17
18	19	20	21	22	23	24
25	26	27	28	29	30	

OCTOBER

M	T	W	T	F	S	S
						1
2	3	4	5	6	7	8
9	10	11	12	13	14	15
16	17	18	19	20	21	22
23	24	25	26	27	28	29
30	31					

NOVEMBER

M	T	W	T	F	S	S
		1	2	3	4	5
6	7	8	9	10	11	12
13	14	15	16	17	18	19
20	21	22	23	24	25	26
27	28	29	30			

DECEMBER

M	T	W	T	F	S	S
				1	2	3
4	5	6	7	8	9	10
11	12	13	14	15	16	17
18	19	20	21	22	23	24
25	26	27	28	29	30	31

Notes

Notes

ABOUT THE AUTHOR

George Petting

Yasmin Boland was born in Germany and grew up in Hobart, Tasmania. After university, she worked as a newspaper journalist, which led her from Tasmania to 'mainland' Australia and eventually to London, where she worked as a journalist and radio and TV producer. In the 1990s, Yasmin learned how to meditate, which completely changed her life. It also opened her up to astrology, which started as a hobby but eventually became her full-time job.

Yasmin is now one of the most widely read astrology writers on the planet. She loves all astrology but has a special interest in the Moon, and specifically in New and Full Moons. At her website yasminboland.com you can read her Daily Moon Message, along with her weekly, monthly and annual horoscopes. Yasmin is the bestselling author of *Moonology*™, *Moonology*™ *Oracle Cards*, *Astrology Made Easy* and *The Mercury Retrograde Book*.

f yasminbolandsmoonology

𝕏 @yasminboland

 @moonologydotcom
@planetyasminboland

moonology.com and **yasminboland.com**